Creative Approaches to CBT

CREATIVE
APPROACHES TO
CBT

ART ACTIVITIES FOR EVERY STAGE
OF THE CBT PROCESS

PATRICIA SHERWOOD

Jessica Kingsley *Publishers*
London and Philadelphia

Disclaimer: No case studies in this book are personal or individual. They are composties developed from a range of experiences with clients and represent themes of experience not individuals' experiences.

First published in 2018
by Jessica Kingsley Publishers
73 Collier Street
London N1 9BE, UK
and
400 Market Street, Suite 400
Philadelphia, PA 19106, USA

www.jkp.com

Copyright © Patricia Sherwood 2018
Internal illustrations of sequences © Tara Sherwood 2018

Library of Congress Cataloging in Publication Data
Names: Sherwood, Patricia, author.
Title: Creative approaches to CBT : art activities for every stage of the CBT process / Patricia Sherwood.
Description: Philadelphia : Jessica Kingsley Publishers, 2018. | Includes bibliographical references and index.
Identifiers: LCCN 2018006130 | ISBN 9781785925085 (alk. paper)
Subjects: | MESH: Cognitive Therapy--methods | Art Therapy--methods
Classification: LCC RC489.C63 | NLM WM 425.5.C6 | DDC 616.89/1425--dc23 LC record available at https://lccn.loc.gov/2018006130

British Library Cataloguing in Publication Data
A CIP catalogue record for this book is available from the British Library

ISBN 978 1 78592 508 5
eISBN 978 1 78450 891 3

Printed and bound in Great Britain

To all clinical mental health workers who work at the interface of human mental health with all its challenges and rewards that they may be inspired to facilitate clients to find new ways of expressing, and transforming their experiences on the pathway to rejuvenation and mental health recovery.

Especially to Gomathi for her vision, hard work and persistence in creating new opportunities for mental health workers to integrate creative therapies into their counselling and clinical work and for inspiring me to write this book.

Contents

1

INTRODUCING CREATIVE APPROACHES TO CBT

Cognitive behavioural therapy (CBT) has as its strength controlled, directed, rational, logical, verifiable interventions that can be researched to provide evidence-based interventions. While much has been documented on verbal strategies compatible with CBT, little has been presented on creative non-verbal strategies compatible with the principles of CBT. Gray (2015) notes the potential for developing creative art-based approaches to CBT. Developing his suggestion, this work elucidates innovative creative approaches and explicitly identifies how they fit within, and can be used by, the CBT compendium of social skills training, visualisation, cognitive restructuring, desensitisation, reinforcement and relapse prevention. These approaches complement verbal strategies to assist clients in acquiring the required skills, and behavioural outcomes, within the CBT model.

To date, creative therapies incorporated by cognitive behavioural therapists have been used peripherally. Colouring in pictures for children, or pre-set mandalas for older clients (Cunningham 2010; McNeil 2011) are such examples, and it is assumed they relax clients or create a more informal therapeutic atmosphere. Other artistic exercises used are often fairly superficial, such as drawing lists or maps of change processes, often not particularly creative but more perfunctory. They usually consist of worksheets with given artistic shapes that the clients fill or colour in. *The CBT Art Activity Book* (Guest 2016) epitomises this approach, as does Lowenstein's book *Creative CBT Interventions for Children with Anxiety* (2016). While there is definitely a role for such art activities in CBT, they remain superficial adjuncts to the CBT process. They do not become in-depth interventions that at their very heart incorporate detailed CBT characteristics, such as tracking bodily sensations, having precise behavioural change goals, utilising reinforcers and repetition in establishing new social skills, and cognitive restructuring and reframing. There are no clearly defined processes for artistic pre- and post-interventions that are repeatable by different therapists with different clients in a range of different environments; as a result, creative therapy has traditionally remained a random adjunct to the CBT model of therapy.

This book presents innovative creative therapeutic approaches that are integral to the CBT approach, characterised by the following five conditions:

1. clear theoretical rational of how the exercise relates to the core principles of CBT

2. precise behavioural goals of the exercises

3. specific outlines and step-by-step instructions for the exercises

4. exercises that are repeatable across a wide range of clients in a wide range of therapy settings

5. clear pre- and post-interventions, in most cases observable through changes of breathing within clients.

The exercises described in this book are compatible with the CBT focus on one of the following: bodily sensations, behavioural change, reinforcers, repetition, imagery suggestions, behavioural activation strategies, social skills, behavioural experiments, desensitisation and cognitive restructuring. These creative processes will provide expanded tools for therapists particularly when working with challenging clients or when seeking more sensory methods for facilitating client engagement and change in the therapeutic process.

These creative approaches to CBT focus on the here and now, looking at the present moment and the contribution to the presenting issue expressed through the client's behaviours, bodily sensations, thoughts and emotions (Ivey et al. 2002). In addition, they offer repeatable sequences that once mastered can be applied across a range of clients in a diversity of situations. In clay, for example, there is a sequence for anger, one for grief and loss, one for speaking up for oneself, and a sequence for releasing guilt. These sequences have a number of repeatable steps, usually three to five, and can be conducted by the therapist and taught to the client to repeat outside of the therapeutic environment if required. In fact, some therapeutic issues such as grief and loss recovery, for example, have a three-stage sequence, which the client repeats over 21 days using watercolour, or clay depending on their preferences. This repetition done every day acts as a strong predictor of behavioural change, a core tenet of CBT. In addition, it reinforces not just a positive transformative thinking process but also one that is reflected in bodily actions so that the likelihood of the new behaviour being sustained is increased. This is elucidated by some of the latest neurolinguistic research:

> Daniel Casasanto of the Max Planck Institute for Psycholinguistics in Nijmegen and Katinka Dijkstra of Erasmus University in Rotterdam investigate embodied cognition – how the body shapes mental activity – and they have already found ways in which our thoughts are influenced by the shape and form of the body. ...in 2007, Dijkstra showed that assuming the body posture associated with a particular experience can aid recall of the memories of that experience. These studies hint at the embodiment of abstract concepts... (Mo 2010)

The creative approaches presented in this book engage the body in new shapes and movements to reflect the new positive behaviour change whether utilising drawing, clay, movement, gesture, breathing, or drama, and contribute to the embodiment of the new desirable behaviour if repeated regularly.

Modelling of new social skills is effected through these creative approaches to CBT sequences which, when repeated daily, facilitate behavioural and cognitive change in the client's life. The development of new social skills, core to the CBT process, while taught in the therapeutic session, requires repetitive and continued practice to effect the desired behaviour change. The creative approaches outlined in this book provide ideal concrete, observable, tangible and interesting mediums for the client to practise and ultimately embody behaviour change, so that it is not just verbalised or thought about, but it is manifested in the individual's behaviour.

When the art medium chosen is particularly meaningful to the client, then the positive rewards of completing daily exercises result in a process of behavioural activation where the reinforcer consolidates the desired behavioural change. The translation from thought to behaviour, from words to behaviour, is a problem that many therapists face, especially in the clinical environment of today with scarce resources and limited numbers of therapy sessions per client. These creative sequences give the client the opportunity to embody a behaviour by practising behavioural change expressed through an art medium on a regular and repetitive basis. They also provide precise and focused interventions to consolidate cognitive reframing and restructuring that is at the heart of many CBT sessions and to extinguish maladaptive self-talk over time.

Finally, some of these creative sequences facilitate clients in the process of desensitisation to trauma, particularly the sequences related to entering into a trauma and exiting a trauma. They are bodily based and tracked through the body by sensing into the stressed parts of the body, where breathing is contracted. They give the client the ability to establish control over the traumatic experience so that they cease gradually to be re-traumatised by the experience. They provide precise steps for entering into the trauma, re-experiencing the trauma and exiting the trauma, and then transforming it with the new information acquired through the bodily experiences of these memories. Thus they are a powerful adjunct to exposure and desensitisation therapies undertaken by some cognitive behavioural therapists.

The following chapters set out precise therapeutic sequences using different artistic mediums that facilitate the goals and principles of CBT and add to the diversity of techniques and tools used by therapists to achieve their goals.

2

DIAGNOSTIC PROCESSES

INTRODUCTION

CBT has a strong commitment to diagnosis in therapy and has developed a battery of verbal diagnostic processes. The creative diagnostic processes described in this chapter are presented as an adjunct tool to some of these verbal processes. They provide a sensory method for obtaining some types of information from clients, particularly from clients who are reserved or reluctant to talk. They are also particularly appropriate for use with children and adolescents. Of course, they can also be used for all clients who respond positively to the particular creative medium used in each exercise. A sample of diagnostic exercises, drawing on the practices of art therapy and clay therapy, are outlined here.

DIAGNOSIS WITH CHILDREN USING COLOURING-IN

BODY MAP SEQUENCE

With small children, it is often difficult to identify the origins of the problem from the child's perspective. It is common in this day of rapid change for young children to present with anxiety. For example, a five-year-old presents with anxiety about going to school but they are unable to explain the cause of the anxiety. The immediate quest is to narrow down the potential anxious behaviour to either the classroom or the playground. Similarly, there are many cases of young children in today's world of rising divorces presenting in therapy with anxiety or stress related issues at home, that both parents believe are caused by the other parent. The child either does not know what is causing the anxiety or is unwilling to say for fear of alienating one or both parents.

Body mapping is a very useful creative art-based tool that can immediately and clearly point to the cause of the problem, so that the therapist can focus the interventions more accurately. It can usually be used with children under the age of ten. This exercise will help develop a creative representation of how the client experiences anxiety in two different environments.

Materials

- one box of crayons

- three sheets of A4 or A3 paper

Directions

Step 1: Ask the child to choose a colour to represent each of the following feelings: sad, bad, happy, scared and angry. On a sheet of paper write down each feeling in the colour the child has chosen. If the child does not yet read, draw 'smiley' icon faces in the chosen colour for each expression.

Chart of feelings and associated colours

Step 2: Explain to the child how feelings are stored in our bodies so that we might be scared in our heart and hands, but be sad in our feet and feel angry in our head.

Step 3: Give the child a gingerbread outline of a human body on an A4 sheet of paper and ask them to colour how they feel in Environment A (in school playground, for example, or Parent 1's home, depending on the presenting issue). They are directed to use colours that they have chosen from their chart of feelings and associated colours.

Body map of feelings at school

Step 4: Then give them the second sheet of paper with a gingerbread outline of a human body and ask them to colour it all in with how they feel in Environment B (such as in the classroom or Parent 2's home). Make sure that the first drawing is not visible while they are drawing the second piece.

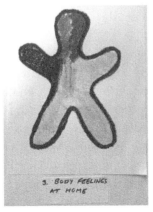

Body map of feelings at home

Step 5: One can then compare the two drawings with the different feelings that the child experiences in their body in Environment A with those feelings in Environment B. This enables the therapist to narrow the focus of the behavioural issue or problem down to the particular environment that is triggering the presenting behaviour, and to do this sufficiently to be able to help produce changes in the behaviour.

Case study

In the example above, the presenting child was five years old and was demonstrating a range of anxiety behaviours, but was unable to communicate to the parent what was causing the problem. It was a clear indicator from the above body maps that the school was the most likely source of the anxiety. Further investigation into the school environment did reveal that the child was not coping with the school learning environment and was failing at tasks other children were succeeding with and was clearly experiencing the environment as overly demanding and feeling 'bad' at school.

Further testing revealed that the child had sensory-processing issues, and when these were addressed the concerning behaviours reduced. Body mapping of feelings is a critical therapeutic art technique to which children under the age of ten respond well. Children are very aware of bodily sensations resulting from feelings of sadness, anger, aloneness, happiness, fear and shame/badness, and, when given the opportunity to express this connection through drawing, do so in most cases very spontaneously.

There is an increasing body of research connecting bodily sensations with particular feelings. Bergland (2014) reports on recent research that clearly links emotional responses to bodily states titled 'Bodily maps of emotions' published in the *Proceedings of the National Academy of Sciences*. This cross-cultural study engaged over 700 participants. Beginning with Candice Pert's *Molecules of Emotion* in 1997, there has been increasing experimental evidence regarding mind–body connections, which children seem to be particularly aware of. Increasingly the mind–body connection is being demonstrated in research in biomedicine, biophysiology and somatic therapies.

Breath is the mediator of the body–mind experience, and it is particularly observable in gesture. The creative exercises presented below using clay demonstrate how gesture reflects emotive experiences stored in the body. These clay therapy interventions are designed to assist the diagnostic process in children, adolescents, and clients who prefer to express themselves through sensory materials.

DIAGNOSIS USING CLAY

FAMILY OF ORIGIN DIAGNOSTIC SEQUENCE

This is an exercise to develop a deeply experienced depiction of the client's relationship with key members of his/her family of origin.

Materials

- working board about half a metre by half a metre

- a water spray bottle

- an airtight bucket of standard pottery clay in one of the earth hues

- towel for cleaning hands

- at least 2 kg of clay

- implements for cutting or carving the clay, such as wooden knife, pencil or clay work tools

Note: Any jewellery, and particularly rings, will need to be removed.

Directions

Step 1: Ask the client to make the number of hand-sized round balls of clay representing significant family members who were/are present in their family of origin. Add an extra ball to represent the client.

Step 2: Begin by asking the client to think of their father and an experience that was typical or is typical of their relationship. This father may be biological or adoptive. If more than one father, then the client completes a piece for each one.

- The client recalls in detail the experience, the physical surroundings and any other physical details.

- The client finds where in their body they feel the strongest sensation as they recall the experience.

- They gesture the feeling in this place in their body with both hands. Does it feel like a knot, a lump, a hollow or some other shape?

- The client takes a piece of clay and shapes it into a form that represents the gesture of the experience of the father that they have sensed.

- When completed the client looks back on the completed piece and notes down the feelings that arise when they look at it.

Step 3: Repeat this exact sequence with each of the significant members of the family one at a time until there is a clay model of experience for each of them. Then ask the client to gesture how they feel when they look at these family members and to make in the last ball of clay the shape of the feelings that they experience.

Step 4: On completion of all of the models of the client's family members, ask the client to arrange the pieces in relationship to each other as they express his/her experience of living in the family system. This then provides a depiction of the family system that gives both the therapist and the client the opportunity to gain new insights and awareness about his/her family system.

Below is an example of this family of origin diagnostic clay sequence completed by a young woman:

Family of origin sequence

In particular, note where the particular members are placed in relation to the client and the shapes of the pieces. In this example, sister represents the client. Are the shapes flowing and upright, representing a bodily experience of relaxation and ease, or are the pieces contracted, hollowed out, crushed and confined, representing the bodily experience of contracted breathing and bodily stress?

Interpretation: Analysing the language of clay forms

Clay shapes and forms contain the three key bodily gestures, which represent how stress and tension are stored in the body or released from the body. These stressors are stored by contractions and restrictions in the breathing so that the client does not breathe in a flowing relaxed manner. There are three polarities, which represent the flow of the breathing in the human body: gravity and levity, contraction and expansion, concavity and convexity. They portray graphically the behavioural gestures of the human emotional and cognitive experiences. The polarities are essential to understand to make some diagnostic conclusions. They are illustrated below:

The three polarities of breathing reflected in gesture

Gravity and levity: Gravity reflects the behavioural states of depression, despair and being burdened and overwhelmed by the weight of circumstances or responsibilities. It is not a healthy state as it reflects the client's feeling of being overtaken by life's cares. Levity contrasts strongly with gravity and reflects the gesture of energy, achievement and happiness. It is much healthier when the client represents themselves in gestures of levity or uprightness. Of course, extreme levity would reflect mania, so the middle point between gravity and levity reflects balance in the bodily behaviours and sensations of breathing.

Contraction and expansion: Contraction is represented by arms and legs crossed in a restricted space. The bodily gesture represents retreat from intimacy with another person and/or life in the world. There is little space to breathe, little space for the client, and it indicates poor boundaries and insufficient personal space to be who you are capable of being. In contrast, expansion reflects the opening out of the arms, the embracing, welcoming warming gesture of expanding waves of joy and happiness and life. This is the gesture of 'I can be who I am.' There is room for me to celebrate who I am and to share my life. The breath moves freely and without restraint. There is the sense of being confident in the world.

Concavity and convexity: Concavity reflects the hollowing out sense of being undermined by life. There is shallow restricted breathing and sense of emptiness in the client's life. It reflects low self-esteem. Convexity represents the state of total exposure, of confident vulnerability, of freedom to expose who you are to the world. The breath is expanding and reaching beyond one's boundaries. There is a sense of exhilaration and of self-confidence.

All these archetypal forms combine in each clay piece to capture a particular bodily emotional experience of pain or pleasure, triumph or defeat, sense of self-flourishing or collapse of space for self. They present poignantly and powerfully a penetrating visual portrayal of the behavioural and emotional states of the client, and they are observed through the shapes of the body created by the client. This is the heart of clay therapy. It becomes a medium to make the inner cognitive and emotional experience visible, known and tangible, revealed through the expression of bodily gestures (Sherwood 2004).

EMPATHY CLAY DIAGNOSTIC SEQUENCE

This exercise will help develop accurate empathetic listening skills and identify the client's ability to demonstrate empathy by accessing their capacity to separate out their feelings from another person's feelings.

Materials

- two working boards about half a metre by half a metre

- a water spray bottle

- an airtight bucket of standard pottery clay in one of the earth hues

- towel for cleaning hands

- three good hand-sized balls of clay for each partner

- implements for cutting or carving the clay

Note: Any jewellery, and particularly rings, will need to be removed.

Directions

Have two persons in conflict or with unresolved communication sit face to face. Agreement on the conflict point or difference is established. One is chosen to begin and takes the role of storyteller and the other takes the role of listener. The listener is the one who is demonstrating through this exercise their capacity for empathy.

Step 1: To sculpture in clay the shape representing the general feeling of the story recounted by the storyteller.

- The storyteller recounts the incident for five minutes.

- The listening partner senses into the general feeling of the story.

- The listening partner, upon completion of the story, selects a ball of clay and makes their first and immediate response to the feelings in the story in clay.

Step 2: To sculpture in clay the shape representing the feelings of the person telling the story.

- The storyteller again recounts the incident for five minutes.

- The listening partner senses into the storyteller's feeling about the story.

- The listening partner, upon completion of the story, selects a ball of clay and makes the storyteller's feeling in clay (this reflects the capacity for empathy).

Step 3: To sculpture in clay the shape representing the listener's response to the story.

- The storyteller recounts the incident for the third time for five minutes.

- The listening partner senses into his/her own feelings about the story.

- The listening partner, upon completion of the story, selects a ball of clay and makes his/her own feeling response to the story in clay.

Interpretation

On completion of all three sculptures, the counsellor asks the storyteller which one of the pieces most closely resembles their feelings about the story they have told. If the storyteller chooses the second piece, this indicates that the listener can enter into another person's feelings and that they have a good level of accurate empathy. If the storyteller chooses the first piece, then this indicates that the listener tends to immediately sense into another person's feelings and could be overly empathetic. If the storyteller selects the final piece, this indicates that the listener has difficulty sensing into another person's feelings accurately and distinguishing them from his/her own feelings.

Now proceed to repeat the above exercises but on this occasion, the roles are reversed. The listener becomes the storyteller who is telling their story, and the person who was previously the storyteller now becomes the listener and has to make their responses to the story in clay three times.

Case study

The sequence in this case study was completed by a young couple who were in conflict over their social life. The storyteller felt that his partner spent too much time socialising with other people. The purpose of the exercise was to assist this non-communicative couple empathise with each other's feelings. The storyteller told about his sadness in the situation and his partner (the listener) made the clay responses. When asked to represent the overall feeling of his experience, her first piece was the broken heart. When he retold the same experience, she was asked to make a piece that represented just his feelings, which was an eye crying. When he retold his experience for the third time, she was asked to make in clay just her feelings, which is represented by an angel wanting freedom to fly and spread her wings. The three pieces are illustrated below:

Empathy development exercise

The storyteller chose the first piece as representing his feelings most accurately, demonstrating that the listener's first response to a situation is very empathetic, overly empathetic. The storyteller also saw the second piece as reflecting his feelings and this demonstrates that the listener has good empathy with another person's experience. The storyteller did not identify with the last piece as his primary feeling which is to be expected, as it was intended to reflect the listener's feelings not the storyteller's feelings. This illustrated in this case that the listener could distinguish her feelings from the other person's feelings.

Following this exchange, they would swap roles, with the listener becoming the storyteller and vice versa. This swap is not illustrated but it follows the same sequence of steps as identified and outlined above.

Most importantly this exercise opened up communication between the couple as she was now able to see the depth of his feeling of loss when she chose to socialise with others, and he was able to understand her desire to be free in her young life and not be controlled by another person's needs.

Reflections and discussion

The clay medium creates very concrete images of the ability to identify accurately feelings in a highly visible way. When working with two people, it is good to focus the exercise on a key issue in which they are having differences in understanding each other's feelings. The exercise will usually take one hour to complete. If one person has particular difficulty identifying another person's feelings in the clay exercise, then the exercise also can be repeated with different issues and different persons, until the listener is more able to respond accurately in clay form to the storyteller's experience. Thus it is an exercise that facilitates the development of empathy in a client.

This exercise also gives the therapist a clear indication as to whether the client is accurately empathetic, overly empathetic or has restricted ability for empathy. It is a tool that also assists in diagnosing when a client needs to practise developing empathy skills.

CONCLUSION

The creative exercises presented in this chapter provide examples of adjunct diagnostic tools in two different mediums that can facilitate the diagnosis of particular behavioural presentations in therapy and provide a creative approach to diagnosis in CBT.

3

SELF-REGULATION AND RELAXATION

INTRODUCTION

Bell (2016) defines self-regulation as being in 'control [of oneself] by oneself'. Self-regulation refers to a system of taking the necessary steps to restore balance in the face of discord, disturbance, disharmony and disequilibrium. This means an individual recognising that they are disturbed and taking appropriate steps to restore their sense of balance, harmony and well-being. In somatic psychotherapy, self-regulation refers to the complex capacities of a human being to restore a state of balance in the face of the ongoing changes and challenges that impact upon them and their environments. Someone who has good emotional self-regulation identifies likely triggers within themselves, and reads early warning signs of emotions in their mind and body accurately. They have a strategic depth in their thinking that gives them the space to make skilful choices to manage their emotions and cognitions so that they do not adversely impact upon themselves or other persons in their environments. They resist impulsive and reactive behaviours, can self-soothe and demonstrate high levels of resilience. They have a flexible range of emotional and behavioural responses to diverse situations and unpredicted changes that are compatible with the demands of their environment. People are able to improve their emotional self-regulation over time through acquiring new skills, developing self-awareness and modelling new behaviours. Perry (n.d.) describes the contribution of somatically based therapy to self-regulation:

> The fundamental goal of somatically based psychotherapy is to restore healthy self-regulation, resilience, and the capacity to be fully present

in the moment. By integrating somatic tools into therapy, it is possible to work directly with symptoms 'where they live' – in the person's body and nervous system. Over time, these efforts to restore self-regulation allow the person to move on with their life, stronger and more resilient than ever.

In this chapter, a selection of exercises will be presented that are drawn from the creative therapies that facilitate self-regulation in clients including children and adolescents.

GROUNDING
Restoring breathing throughout the body

Contracted and restricted breathing is an observable indicator of stress in the human body, and it is reflected in gesture, emotional outbursts and stress experienced physically as well as in a range of emotional disorders, particularly anxiety conditions and depression. When someone is happy and contented, the breath is observed to flow freely and is reflected in gestures of expansiveness, equilibrium and lightness. Self-regulation is easy to achieve when one is in a fully upright breathing position and much more challenging to achieve when the breathing is contracted. To self-regulate one's emotions, mindfulness, or being fully aware of the present moment and the surrounding variables, is essential. There is a strategic depth at these times of mindfulness to review behavioural choices and to eliminate dysfunctional internal dialogue.

'Grounding', or the idea of breathing fully into the body, was a term developed by Lowen (1976) in his bioenergetics work. Grounding is the process of teaching clients to breathe fully into their body by focusing on their feet being firmly planted on the floor and moving into a range of bodily gestures that help them relax into their body. Lowen proposed that we need to reconnect the client more fully with their body, for therapy to succeed, and that alienation from self and others begins with estrangement from one's own body. It is only through fully occupying our body that we can be in touch with self, others and the world, rather than living from a dissociated mind state, or a feeling state that is at the root of all powerlessness, fear, depression and anxiety.

Identifying not being grounded or fully present throughout one's body

The symptoms of a person who is not grounded or present need to be identified by therapists to avoid wasting time and to ensure that the client maximises their learning in the session. These symptoms include lack of focus either by 'day dreaming' or being scattered in one's thinking. Often not feeling grounded affects facial expressions and gestures and produces a glazed or distant look in the eyes, fidgeting, foot tapping and shaking in parts of the body. Not being grounded or present can be camouflaged by the client talking excessively, often rapidly and repeating the same thing over and over again, avoiding any real contact with the reality of their feelings. Even when the client gives an appropriate response, there is the overwhelming feeling that they are not present or listening. It could be described metaphorically as 'the lights are on but no one is home'.

When someone is not present, they will not remember the details of what has occurred, so the therapeutic encounter is of very limited value. It is our primary job as therapists to ensure that the client is fully present and breathing well before commencing therapeutic interventions. It is good to begin by assisting clients who are not present or grounded, particularly clients who have anxiety or anger issues, to identify in their bodies the process of not being present to the world. It occurs progressively, but clients are more aware of certain parts of the progression than others depending on their own self-awareness. A client stops being present to the degree in which they become stressed and contract their breathing. This is reflected in the body as follows:

1. Often the client experiences shaking legs or feet as the breath contracts in the lower part of the body first.

2. The client may feel the need to go to the toilet when breath contracts in the abdomen and the 'gut' feels stressed, or may simply feel tension in the abdomen.

3. Breath is contracted up to the stomach, and clients feel that they have 'butterflies in the stomach' or feel like vomiting.

4. The breath is contracted in the throat, and at this point the person often feels panicky or unable to breathe freely.

5. When the breath is so constricted that it is contracted into the head, particularly through the forehead, the person feels dizzy.

6. When the breath rapidly contracts throughout the body right up to the crown of the head such as in sudden shock, then fainting may occur.

GROUNDING SEQUENCE

Exercise 1

This exercise of 'grounding' is particularly applicable to children in states of anger or fear and assists them to return to calmness and restore full breathing again in their body. However, it is suitable for all adults as well, if they are willing to practise it regularly and apply this exercise when they have learned to notice the identified symptoms of contracting breathing and not being present to themselves and their lives.

Directions

Step 1: Notice that you are angry or frightened and where in your body you feel these feelings.

Step 2: Sense how these feelings contract your breathing. Does it feel like a lump, a knot, a hard rock, a twist or some other shape?

Step 3: Stamp both feet on the ground and walk around the room saying aloud in unison with the steps of your feet, 'I am here, I am safe, I am here, and I am safe.'

Step 4: Keep repeating these words while stamping your feet until you feel calm and feel that you are breathing deeply again.

Exercise 2

An alternative fun exercise that achieves the same results with children is to get a drum and have them march around the room beating the drum while repeating, 'I am here, I am safe, I am protected' in rhythm with the drum, or some other rhyme in unison with the beating and marching rhythm that supports their feelings of safety. Continue this behavioural intervention until the feelings of fear, anxiety or anger have diminished.

Exercise 3

In reality, any aerobic activity (exercising, using a gym treadmill or bike vigorously, running for an extended period of time and playing ball sports) that produces deep breathing will 'ground' the client and cause them to become more aware of their bodily sensations and behaviour. They can then choose behavioural options that are skilfully orientated to meet the demands of their environment and the space and equipment available.

DIAGNOSING AND TRANSFORMING ANGER

Anger management issues are one of the major presenting issues in therapy in children, adolescents and adults. Anger is always the smoke that camouflages the log of fear that actually causes the anger. Anger is the fight response in the face of a perceived threat. It is a complicated phenomenon because anger may be externalised (aggressive) and so affect others directly, or internalised (passive) and implode within the individual's body causing ill health and secondary indirect expression such as sarcasm, bitchiness, gossip, revenge, manipulation and lying. However, regardless of whether it is overtly expressed or covertly expressed, anger contracts the breathing within the body and produces stress and lack of mindfulness, which results in poor self-regulation.

IDENTIFYING ANGER

This simple therapeutic art exercise awakens individuals to the early-warning signs of anger and helps them develop more awareness around the anger-management process. The first step in controlling anger is to know what it looks like, just like the first step for not having an accident at the traffic lights is to know that red means stop. This exercise is done using crayons and paper as well as body movement.

Materials

- A4 paper

- oil crayons or acrylic paints (or clay, depending on the client's preference)

Directions

Step 1: Stand up and practise breathing down to your toes.

Step 2: Breathe down to the tips of your toes until you can imagine your breath coming out of the tips of your toes. Take four to five deep breaths and during each breath imagine that the breath is gradually spreading through the whole body down to the extremities. Stamp your feet so that you feel that you are drawing the breath down to the very soles of your feet.

Step 3: Think of a time when you were angry and watch where in your body the angry feeling lives. It will feel uncomfortable and stressed or tense in that part of your body.

Step 4: Place your hand on that part of your body where the tension feels strongest.

Step 5: Draw the shape of the tense or stressed feeling with your crayons on white paper. Is it like a knot, a black lump of stone, is it like a ball of string? Or some other shape? Alternatively, you could make the shape of the lump in clay.

Step 6: This is the anger inside of you. Once you feel it, you know that you are angry. This occurs before you express the anger towards others or your environment. It is the orange light warning you that you need to take action to stop now.

FIRST AID: RELEASING ANGER

This exercise drawn from drama therapy is known as 'exiting or bamboo' (see also Chapter 8) and was developed by Tagar (1996).

Directions

Step 1: Stand up and close your eyes and breathe down to your toes. Make sure no one is in front of you. It is ideal if you can face the wall, a window or an open door.

Step 2: Place your hand on the part of your body that feels uncomfortable, tense, stressed and angry.

Step 3: Collect the tense or angry feeling into a ball with your hands and throw it as far away as possible. As you throw it away make a loud, hard 'g' sound.

Step 4: Take a step backwards and stamp your feet hard.

Step 5: Shake off the angry feeling by shaking both hands vigorously.

Step 6: Repeat Steps 2–5, three to five times or more until you no longer feel the tension or anger in your body.

IDENTIFYING THE CAUSE OF ANGER AND RELEASING IT

Anger is only a symptom camouflaging a deep inner wounding. Anger is simply smoke. The real fire is the deep-seated experience of fear within that triggers the anger. The deep-seated fear needs to be addressed. Only then will anger not continue to arise. Until the cause can be identified and the healing of the underlying fear effected, one cannot expect any lasting change in behaviour.

This exercise uses clay, which is a wonderful substance for working with anger because it absorbs anger allowing the client to mould it, shape it, beat it, punch it, squeeze it or flatten it (Henley 2002). In *The Healing Art of Clay Therapy* (Sherwood 2004) the therapeutic efficacy of working with clay with clients with anger is well documented.

Materials

- working board about half a metre by half a metre
- a water spray bottle
- an airtight bucket of standard pottery clay in one of the earth hues
- towel for cleaning hands
- three good hand-sized balls of clay
- implements for cutting and carving the clay

Note: Any jewellery, and particularly rings, will need to be removed.

Directions

The overall sequence has four parts, which are diagrammatically illustrated below:

The four parts of the anger clay therapy sequence

Steps 1, 2 and 3 are diagnostic, seeking to find the cause or trigger to the angry behaviour. Step 4 represents the intervention. In between Steps 3 and 4, there is an intermediate intervention process that will be identified and detailed within the sequence as it is presented below.

Step 1: To express the exploded anger (the smoke)…

- Recall a situation where you exploded your anger. Remember the details of the persons, the setting, the time, the incident of dispute.

- Sense into the part of your body that is most uncomfortable when you recall this incident.

- Place your hand on that part of the body.

- Step forward into that part of your body.

- Sense into the anger and capture it with your hands.

- Explode it against a wall with a loud 'g' or '*ahh*'.

- Repeat several times until you can see the shape of your exploded anger dripping down the wall and feel that you can now breathe deeply.

- Exit and make the shape of the anger in clay.

If the anger is not clearly exploded, repeat Step 1 until it is exploded. Imploded anger may be created as a block, a round ball, a flat block, a solid. Exploded anger will appear when the clay is fragmented into pieces or spread out across the table, or has tentacles or arrow-like arms emerging from it in a number of directions. If it remains in a tight ball or a solid shape, then keep repeating the explosion above, until the client can release their contracted breathing and see the exploded anger clearly.

Exploded anger (the smoke)

Step 2: To locate the place of suffering: the torture chamber (the fire)...

- Enter again into the place in your body where the anger is experienced.

- This time, sense backwards to the time before you explode. This is the place where the pressure builds up before you explode.

- Feel the pressure build up in this place.

- Sense how your body feels trapped in this place of stress and contracted breathing. Is it like being caught between a vice, in a prison, under a rock, in the middle of a concrete block, etc.?

- Exit from this place by stepping backwards and make the shape of the place in which you are trapped in clay, which is called 'the trap' or the place of suffering. It is experienced like a torture chamber before the individual explodes because it is here that the breath is tightly contracted.

The trap – trapped in a locked box

There are many different types of traps but if you ask the client to point to where they are trapped in the piece that they have made, they can clearly tell you that they are under the shape, or inside the shape or in some way contained by the shape that they have made in clay. This prevents them feeling free and contracts their breathing.

Step 3: To uncover the 'trapped or fearful one', the cause of the anger (the log of wood that fuels the fire to burn and create smoke)…

- Enter back into the place of the body where the anger has been sensed.

- Step into the trapped place where one's breathing is contracted.

- Gesture with your whole body how you are trapped in the torture chamber; for example, crouch down or lie on the ground or curl up into a ball, or engage whatever gesture you body needs to take to fit into the trapped shape you have made in Step 2.

- Sense the shape of your body and identify the feelings you have when your body is in this shape.

- Sense into your earliest memory of your body being in this shape.

- Exit and make the shape of the trapped gesture in clay.

- Note down your feelings and your earliest memory of your body being in this shape.

Step 3 uncovers the cause of the anger. The trapped or fearful one has been attempting to protect itself with a primitive defence of anger. This stage becomes the focus for the healing of this particular manifestation of anger. It is really the pre-intervention representation in clay as the previous steps have been diagnostic and have now led the therapist and the client to observe the cause of the anger. One can observe how crushed the fearful one is and how unable to breathe as their gesture reflects.

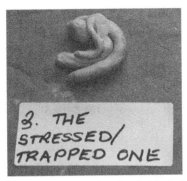

The stressed/trapped one (the log that fuels the fire)

The intervention

It is clear that an intervention is required in order to release the stress and contracted breathing in the body of the client as discovered in Step 3, because this is the one that is driving the angry behaviour. Anger is a camouflage for its fear and distress.

It is best to undertake this process by first asking the client to return to the gesture literally that they have made in clay, and tell the therapist whether they feel attacked or abandoned, or both, when they are crouched or curled up that gesture. If they say abandoned, then complete the resourcing or self-soothing process below. If they say attacked, then complete the empowering process also outlined in the following pages. If they say both then complete both sequences with the attacking sequence first.

Resourcing: This is required when the client experiences abandonment, absence or depletion. This may mean absence of love, connectedness, warmth, tenderness, joy, rest, peace or many other qualities. To build recovery here, one needs to bring back the missing qualities to this place by engaging the client and getting them to visualise and recreate the missing quality. This involves using imagery suggestions as follows:

- Name the qualities required by the trapped/fearful one.

- Recall somebody living or dead, known or unknown, who represents the missing quality.

- Imagine what that quality feels like.

- Stand in the gesture of that quality.

- Breathe in that quality into the part of the body where the initial stress was sensed.

- Choose a colour for that quality and breathe in that colour.

- Find a sound for that quality.

- Give yourself that sound.

- Make the shape of the quality in clay.

Repeat the above process for all the missing qualities that the client has named. These qualities are varied and personal. They need to be integrated into a behavioural activation programme after the therapy session. In the illustrated example, the qualities were *friends, love* and *warmth*.

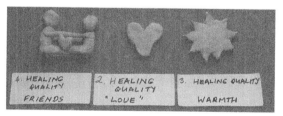

Example of the qualities of protection, love, nurturance, strength surrounding the wounded one.

Empowerment: Alternatively, when the client feels attacked or invaded, an empowerment process is required. Usually the client will feel attacked by the words, actions or behaviour of another person, or situation that has been experienced as an invasion into their personal space. Empowerment is required because through the attack the clients have experienced collapsed boundaries, defeat, abuse and powerlessness, and failed to hold on to a clear personal space. To remove the feeling of attack, ask the client to enter back into the shape of the trapped/fearful one they have made in clay.

- While inside the shape, ask how they feel the force attacks them. Do they feel it is like a hammer, an axe, an arrow, a twisting, a knife?

- Ask the client to step out of the shape and stand up in a new position of strength that represents recovery from defeat. Suggest positive gestures if necessary.

- Ask the client to reverse out the object that has attacked them by making a gesture to remove the object with an associated sound that goes from contracted to expanded. For example, removing the feeling of being stabbed would require the client to gesture removing the knife from their body and throwing it away while accompanying it with a sound like '*Aaaarrrhh!*'. Repeat this gesture of removing the knife and throwing it away until the client feels they can breathe freely again. This will restore the rhythmic flow of breathing.

If the client experiences both being attacked and abandoned then they complete both the empowering and resourcing sequences above.

Step 4: The recovered or calm one that is fully breathing...

- Make the gesture of the new strong empowered position with the body.

- Ask the client to make the image of the new strong fully breathing gesture in clay.

The calm one – example of an empowered one who is
fully breathing and no longer in fear and anger

Interpretation

When the stressed/trapped one is compared with the recovering one, we can see that in this sequence with this client there have been effective changes. From a gesture in the pre-intervention figure, that represents contracted breathing, with concave and gravity as the primary forces, we move to a figure of expansion, levity and convexity representing the gestures in the clay figure of breathing more fully. This transformation is clearly illustrated below.

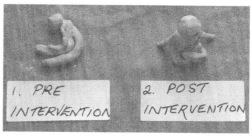

Pre- and post-intervention

Discussion

This clay therapy sequence has been completed with individuals and groups of clients in many cultures of the world including Western European, indigenous Australians, Chinese, Malays, Indians, and black Africans, with similar repeatable results. An illustration of its cross-cultural application is documented in detail in a project undertaken with Rwandan genocide survivors in 2012 (Sherwood and O'Meara 2012). Although the sequence takes some practice for the counsellor to master, once this is achieved it can be completed within an hour and a half. *It should not be attempted until the counsellor is proficient in the first aid exercise, above, so if at any stage the client appears to be overwhelmed, they can be quickly exited to a quiet, peaceful breathing space again.*

CONCLUSION

All sequences documented in this chapter provide a selection of somatically based creative therapy interventions that promote self-regulation of a client's emotional life through their focus on transforming contracted breathing into relaxed non-stressed breathing. Clients can only self-regulate emotions in the degree to which they restore their breathing and thus remain fully present to the immediate situation before them. The importance of breathing as a bridge between body and mind, thoughts, feelings and behaviours cannot be overemphasised. The Vietnamese Buddhist monk and peace activist Thich Nhat Hanh describes it eloquently:

> Breath is the bridge, which connects life to consciousness, which unites your body to your thoughts. Whenever your mind becomes scattered, use your breath as the means to take hold of your mind again. (Thich Nhat Hanh 1987, p.15)

4

VISUALISATION AND GUIDED IMAGERY

INTRODUCTION

Guided imagery therapy is a structured visualisation process and a well established cognitive-behavioural technique in which a client is guided in imagining a particular image or series of experiences with a therapeutic intention to restore skilful and functional cognitive thinking processes. Centred on strengthening the mind–body connection, visualisation processes, particularly if repeated regularly, can have a profound effect on a range of behaviours. Utay and Miller (2006) have comprehensively documented the efficacy of guided imagery techniques across a wide range of issues, including the management of anxiety, anger, behavioural disorders and motivation. There is considerable evidence showing the efficacy of guided image making for specific issues such as asthma (Dobson *et al.* 2005), stress (Rossman 2010), migraine (Ilacqua 1994) and pain (Kabat-Zinn 2013) just to name a few. Guided imagery has been used in a variety of ways in behavioural therapy, as documented in the online *Encyclopedia of Mental Disorders* (www.middisorders.com). They include the following:

- anti-future shock imagery (preparing for a feared future event)

- positive imagery (using pleasant scenes for relaxation training)

- aversive imagery (using an unpleasant image to help eliminate or reduce undesirable behaviour)

- associated imagery (using imagery to track unpleasant feelings)

- coping imagery (using images to rehearse in order to reach a behavioural goal or manage a situation)

- 'step-up' technique (exaggerating a feared situation and using imagery to cope with it).

The following creative CBT techniques use positive imagery in repeatable sequences that promote transformation of negative experiences and cognitive worldviews into positive worldviews, or transform defeated experiences and negative internal dialogues into positive coping worldviews and dialogues:

- the transformation from grief and loss to positive growth

- the transformation from self-condemnation to self-forgiveness

- the transformation from despair to hope

- the transformation from betrayal to trust.

For these visualising exercises, resource files are prepared that contain positive images drawn from ancient as well as contemporary cultural and religious traditions, images from nature, including animals as well as landscapes, images of inspiring people and people expressing positive life qualities. All images are chosen based on the view that they are able to be used to positively reinforce the client's sense of well-being or meet particular needs. As clients come from a wide range of worldviews, images from a range of worldviews and communities are included such as Buddhist, Hindu, Christian, Islamic, Jewish, secular, humanistic and agnostic.

The images are placed in two resource files. File 1 contains images that all share in common a nurturing or sustaining aspect and are particularly appropriate to providing countering images from experiences of abandonment or rejection, aloneness and isolation. In File 2, images share in common the protective element and can inspire clients to invoke protection, strength and boundaries, particularly in the face of the experience of being 'attacked'.

Resource file 1: Nurturing imagery
Motherhood, fatherhood, loving friends, loving partners, soft nurturing images of nature, images of loving human beings known and unknown, nurturing spiritual images, and images of nurturing animals are included in this folder.

Resource file 2: Protective imagery

Warriors, protectors both male and female, fierce animals that can protect and defend, images of strong environments such as mountains, volcanoes, rocks and images of protective spiritual figures and icons are included in this folder. Light images of power and protection are also included.

These folders usually comprise around 100 plus images and equip the therapist with on-the-spot images to cover a very wide range of client preferences and needs, in relation to likely presenting therapeutic issues. They provide a bank of imagery suggestions to facilitate the transformation through limiting negative self-talk and psychological limiting experiences to positive internal dialogue and behavioural change.

THE TRANSFORMATION FROM GRIEF AND LOSS TO POSITIVE COPING

Grief and loss experiences affect all clients in some ways, as in contemporary society, there is so much to lose whether it be death of a friend or family member, loss of employment, an environment, a pet, health or livelihood. In particular, with escalating rates of job mobility, relationship instability and divorces, people daily find themselves dealing with losses. Without skills to keep breathing through the loss and the grief, many people end in depression or despair.

Grief and loss is a process that takes some time to resolve, and this exercise facilitates the movement through the grief and loss process to a place of continuing growth and willingness to engage in the world in a functional manner. The exercise, using guided imagery, is recommended to be completed by clients on a repetitive basis for 21–28 days, and the paintings are kept in a folder and brought to therapy each time the client attends during that period of time.

The objective is to restore relaxed and deep breathing in the client's body because breathing becomes shallow and contracted during grief and loss experiences. We do this in association with guided imagery that provides positive images upon which the client can rebuild positive, functional behaviours. This process also provides a visual process for the client to track changes in their emotions and cognitions around their grief and loss.

This exercise can be completed in watercolour or in clay. In my experience, Indigenous Australians generally prefer clay, as do many males. It is illustrated using watercolour here. Note that watercolour may be more suitable for older people, children, convalescing persons and clients who are not robust physically, and those who are exhausted, have chronic fatigue, are prone to psychosis or who express a preference to work in watercolour rather than clay.

Materials

- watercolour set of paints
- 3 sheets of watercolour paper
- 2 jars of clean water
- 2 paint brushes: one large and one small
- one paint palette for mixing colours

Directions

Step 1: Ask the client to locate in their body where they feel the sadness. Suggest that they sense into the colours and shapes in that part of their body and paint the colours.

Note: To avoid painting of visual pictures, first paint the sheet with clear water then have the client place the colours on the wet paper.

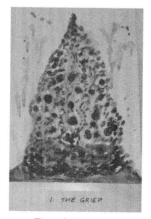

The grief and loss

Step 2: Ask the client to name the quality they feel they have lost when they think of their sadness. Is it joy, friendship, warmth, love, fun, companionship?

- Select an image of someone spiritual or human, living or dead, animal or image from nature who represents the missing quality and ask the client to imagine breathing in this missing quality from them.

- Instruct the client to breathe in the missing quality to that part of their body, then to let the quality flow throughout their whole body.

- The client selects a colour for the missing quality as it flows through their body and draws a picture in colour representing the new flow of breath in the body

The missing healing quality

Step 3: Invite the client to sense how the missing quality is flowing through their breathing. Ask them to paint how the initial place in which they experienced the sadness is starting to change.

The healing place

At the completion of this exercise, it is helpful to discuss with the client strategies for bringing more of the missing quality back into their life. This includes exploring different dimensions of the client's life including social, personal, work and family contexts if relevant. Encourage them to implement one of the strategies before the next session and to complete it in a routine regular pattern. An example is joining a social group of their interest that meets weekly or fortnightly, to deal with their loss of friendship or connectedness. This exercise focuses on changing behaviour through changed lifestyle as well as through the prescribed visualisation exercise.

The client leaves the session with clear instructions in writing of how to repeat the guided imagery watercolour sequence that they have just done in the therapy session. Each day they may choose a different missing quality if that is what is uppermost in their thoughts on that day. They can choose the same quality for several days in a row, if this is dominant in their thinking at the time. Ask the client to date each set of three paintings and place them consecutively in a plastic leafed folder or something similar. It is desirable that they repeat this process for at least seven days, but 21–28 days should be the goal. Another example of this watercolour exercise is illustrated in Sherwood (2008, p.69).

THE TRANSFORMATION FROM SELF-CONDEMNATION TO SELF-FORGIVENESS

This is an excellent sequence using guided imagery to facilitate clients moving from self-condemnation to self-forgiveness. Self-condemnation can be a major psychological obstacle for a client preventing them from moving forward positively in their life. It often lies behind self-sabotaging behaviours such as addictions, and is evident in some sexual abuse cases as well as many other day-to-day life situations. Through negative thinking, the client holds tenaciously to an image of themselves as faulty, inadequate and in some ways hopeless, helpless or useless. This exercise provides alternative imagery suggestions and supports the development of a positive internal dialogue.

This guided imagery sequence provides alternative positive self-forgiving and self-accepting imagery for the client, and if repeated daily for at least seven days it can facilitate the client making transformative changes towards more skilful and functional behaviours towards themselves and others. The self-forgiveness sequence is based on having the client choose images of three figures who could forgive them when they find they cannot forgive themselves.

This exercise can be completed in watercolour, oil crayons or acrylic paint. This is illustrated using oil crayons.

Materials

- 4 sheets of paper suited for the colour medium chosen
- resource folders containing positive images with at least 50 images in total
- art medium of choice, in this case oil crayons.

Directions

Step 1: Where in your body do you feel the self-condemnation? Imagine stepping forward into that part of your body and sense the shape of the breath. Draw the shape in crayon. This is the pre-intervention imprint of self-condemnation.

The unforgivable one

Ask the client to select three images from the resource folder of people who could forgive them. Commonly used persons selected by clients include the Dalai Lama, Nelson Mandela, Mother Teresa, Martin Luther King, Gandhi, Fred Hollows, Thich Nhat Hanh, Sister Chan Khong. Other images often chosen include one's dog, auntie, grandmother or some other forgiving person they have known personally in their life. Place the self-condemnation image in the centre, and around the image the three pictures of the persons or animals that have been chosen who could forgive them. The client in this example chose Christ, Desmond Tutu and their dog.

Three images of forgiveness around the unforgivable one

Step 2: Starting with the first person chosen by the client, begin a positive resourcing sequence with these questions and instructions for the client:

- Where in the body do your experience the need for the missing quality of self-forgiveness?

- Place your hands on that part of your body.

- Visualise the first image that represents the missing quality of self-forgiveness and imagine receiving this missing quality from them.

- Breathe in the missing quality to that part of your body, then let the quality flow throughout your whole body.

- Colour your breath the colour of the missing quality and continue to breathe it in for five minutes.

- Stand in the new gesture of the quality of self-forgiveness[1] that you have just visualised receiving from... [in this example, your dog].

- Find a sound for the missing quality and make the sound aloud. Use a vowel sound if possible as it increases breathing into the body and so helps to relax the physical body. Alternatively think of a song that reminds you of this quality of self-forgiveness.

- Draw a picture in colour representing the new flow of breath of self-forgiveness just received in the body. Place this image next to the picture of your dog.

---

1   This is the shape of your body, particularly your arms, legs and head, that expresses how you feel. There is no right or wrong gesture here, whatever the client chooses to gesture self-forgiveness (or, in the exercises that follow, hope and trust) is acceptable. It is important that the client consciously recognises the shape in their bodily gesture when they focus upon particular emotions.

Quality of self-forgiveness received from my dog

Step 3: Repeat all of the points in Step 2 but this time using the second image chosen by the client to represent self-forgiveness. In this case, the client chose Christ, and the drawing was as follows and was placed next to the image of Christ that the client selected.

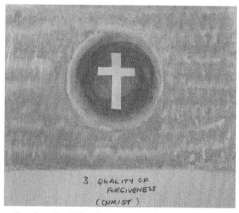

Quality of self-forgiveness received from Christ

Step 4: Repeat all of the points in Step two again but this time using the third image chosen by the client to represent self-forgiveness. In this case, the client chose Archbishop Tutu, and the drawing was as follows and placed next to the image of Desmond Tutu that the client selected.

Quality of self-forgiveness received from Desmond Tutu

Step 5: Now ask the client to place their hands on the same part of the body where the initial self-condemnation was located. Ask them to sense into that part of the body and draw a single large picture showing the flow of energy in that part of the body having now received self-forgiveness from these three persons. This is the post-intervention image that represents the transformation from self-condemnation to self-forgiveness. *Place this on top of the image of self-condemnation* (the unforgivable one).

Post-intervention: the forgiven one

The completed self-forgiveness sequence will look visually like this:

The completed self-forgiveness sequence

Interpretation

The pre-intervention and post-intervention images illustrate how in post-intervention the colours lighten, expand and flow, all signs of the breath returning to the part of the body previously contracted by the self-condemnation. The new images also provide the client with positive enhancing visualisations to support new positive cognitive perceptions of themselves that provide foundational images for positive internal dialogue.

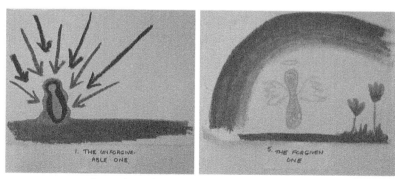

Comparison of pre- and post-intervention images

THE TRANSFORMATION FROM DESPAIR TO HOPE

The epidemic of depression in contemporary society also masks a widespread human condition of despair. In a state of despair, someone has given up on the will to live. They could get out of bed in the morning and face the day but there is no purpose to their life. When people lose their hope and sink into despair this profoundly affects their health and well-being and their desire to create and connect to fulfilling relationships within their communities whether through intimate relationships, family, community, their workplace or the natural environment.

This guided imagery sequence provides alternative, positive, hopeful imagery for the client and, if repeated daily for at least seven days, can facilitate the client making transformative changes to more skilful and functional behaviours towards themselves and others. The despair to hope creation sequence is based on having the client choose images of three figures who should be in despair but who have retained their hope even in the most diffcult and challenging circumstances.

This exercise can be completed in watercolour, oil crayons or acrylic paint. This is illustrated using watercolours.

Materials

- 4 sheets of paper suited for the colour medium chosen

- resource folders containing positive images with at least 50 images in total

Directions

Step 1: Where in your body do you feel the despair? Imagine stepping forward into that part of your body and sense the shape of the breath. Draw the shape in crayon. This is the pre-intervention image of despair.

The despairing one

Ask the client to select three images from the resource folder of people who have demonstrated hope in difficult circumstances and who should be in despair but are not. Commonly used persons selected by clients include the Dalai Lama, Nelson Mandela, Mother Teresa, Martin Luther King, Gandhi, Fred Hollows, Thich Nhat Hanh and Aung San Suu Kyi. Other images often chosen include regenerating nature after a bushfire, a mother after loss of a child that goes on caring and loving her other children, a friend who has survived cancer and worked through the illness with hope. Place the image of despair in the centre and around this the three images of hope selected by the client. The client in this example chose Nelson Mandela, Mother Teresa and regenerating nature. The layout of the selected images around the despairing one is the same as the previous sequence.

Step 2: Starting with the first person chosen by the client, begin a positive resourcing sequence with these questions and instructions for the client:

- Where in the body do your experience the need for the missing quality of hope.

- Place your hands on that part of the body.

- Visualise the first image that represents the missing quality of hope and imagine receiving this missing quality from them.

- Breathe in the missing quality to that part of your body, then let the quality flow throughout your whole body.

- Colour your breath the colour of the missing quality of hope and continue to breathe it in for five minutes.

- Stand in the new gesture of the quality of hope that you have just visualised receiving from... [in this example, Nelson Mandela].

- Find a sound for the missing quality and make the sound aloud. Use a vowel sound if possible as it increases breathing into the body and as such helps to relax the physical body. Alternatively think of a song that inspires you to be hopeful. Play the song or sing it.

- Draw a picture in colour representing the new flow of breath of hope just received in the body. Place this image next to the picture of Nelson Mandela.

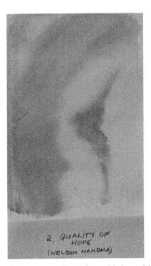

Quality of hope received from Nelson Mandela

Step 3: Repeat all of the points in Step 2 but this time using the second image chosen by the client to represent hope. In this case, the client chose Mother Teresa, and the following painting was placed next to the image of Mother Teresa that the client selected.

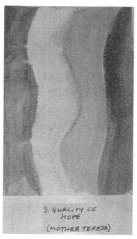

Quality of hope received from Mother Teresa

Step 4: Repeat all of the points in Step 2 again but this time using the third image chosen by the client to represent hope triumphing over despair. In this case, the client chose the hope in nature regenerating after environmental devastation and painted it as follows:

Quality of hope in regenerating nature

Step 5: Now ask the client to place the hand on the same part of the body where the initial despair was located. Ask them to sense into that part of the body and draw a single large picture showing the flow of energy in that part of the body having now received hope from these three persons, in the face of the previously despairing experiences. This is the post-intervention image that represents the transformation from despair to hope.

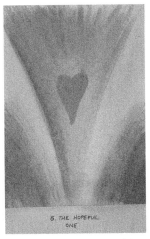

Post-intervention: the hopeful one

Now place the original image on the ground, and the three positive painted images of hope around it. Then place the fifth piece of art, the 'Post-intervention: the hopeful one', over the first piece so that the client now has the overall view of the guided imagery transformation.

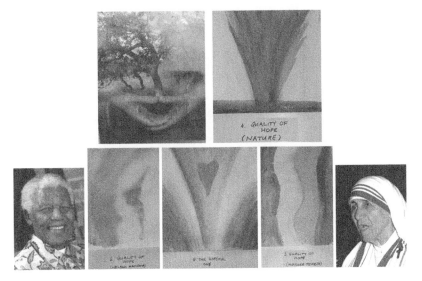

The completed despair to hope sequence

This is the same layout as in the previous sequence from self-condemnation to self-forgiveness. Have the client take a photograph on their phone of this final arrangement and if they so desire they can take the drawings with them to place in a significant place in their home where they can daily renew these images by visualising them and consciously taking a few deep breaths to breathe in these new qualities. It is recommended the client complete this exercise everyday for at least seven days.

Interpretation

The new images provide the client with positive enhancing visualisations to support new positive cognitive perceptions of themselves. The pre-intervention and post-intervention images illustrate how in the post-intervention the colours lighten, expand and flow, all signs of the breath returning to the part of the body previously contracted by the despairing worldview. The dark colours are replaced by bright sunny colours while the flow of the breath is now expressed in clear, free strokes rather than contracted and contorted brush strokes.

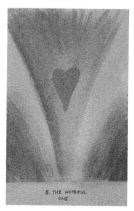

Comparison of pre-and post-intervention images

THE TRANSFORMATION FROM BETRAYAL TO TRUST

Betrayal is a common feeling among broken intimate relationships, divorces, some broken friendships and in some family situations. Often a client who is cognitively focused upon the betrayal has great difficulty letting go of old situations and experiences and living in the present moment. They fail to create new productive and skilful futures for themselves, often living in regret and/or bitterness with very negative internal dialogues.

The betrayal to trust sequence provides the client who has experienced betrayal with new positive imagery associated with trust, so they can move forward into the present moment and create positive internal dialogue and imagery. Initially clients experience betrayal as a force that has attacked them as reflected in the English language: 'a knife in the heart', 'a knife in the back', 'a kick in the stomach'. Clients are asked to visualise, draw, describe, and select an image of how they experience the betrayal in their bodies. If they say a knife in the heart then using gesture and sound, counsellor and client visualise and gesture pulling out the knife from their heart and throwing it away while breathing out and releasing the contracted breathing. We do this several times then breathe deeply back into the part of the body that experienced the 'knife' or whatever force the client describes as having attacked them. This is followed by the betrayal to trust sequence outlined below using guided imagery and redirecting the client's cognitive and behavioural actions towards developing the experience of trust in their lives.

This guided imagery sequence provides alternative positive imagery for the client to facilitate their cognitive and behavioural change from feeling betrayed to being able to trust again. If repeated daily for at least seven days this can facilitate the client making transformative changes towards more skilful and functional behaviours towards themselves and others. The betrayal to trust sequence enables the client to choose three images of persons, animals, archetypes or natural images that they could trust. This sequence follows the same pattern as the preceeding two sequences but focuses instead on the movement from betrayal to trust.

This exercise can be completed in watercolour, oil crayons or acrylic paint. I am illustrating this sequence using crayons.

Materials

- 4 sheets of paper suited for the colour medium chosen
- resource folders containing positive images with at least 50 images in total

Directions

Step 1: Where in your body do you feel the betrayal? Imagine stepping forward into that part of your body and sense the shape of the breath. Draw the shape in crayon. This is the pre-intervention image of betrayal.

The betrayed one

Ask the client to select three images from the resource folder of people who they feel they can trust. Commonly used persons selected by clients include the Dalai Lama, Nelson Mandela, Mother Teresa, Martin Luther King, Gandhi, Fred Hollows, Christ, and Mother Mary. Place the image of betrayal in the centre and around the image the three pictures of the persons whom they can trust. This client chose Mother Mary, her Nana and her dog. The layout of the selected images around the despairing one is the same as the previous sequence.

Step 2: Starting with the first person chosen by the client, begin a positive resourcing sequence with these questions and instructions for the client:

- Where in the body do your experience the need for the missing quality of trust.

- Place your hands on that part of the body.

- Visualise the first image that represents the missing quality of trust and imagine receiving this missing quality from one of the chosen images.

- Breathe into the body the missing quality of trust then let the quality flow throughout your whole body.

- Colour your breath the colour of the missing quality and continue to breathe it in for five minutes

- Stand in the new gesture of the quality of trust that you have just visualised receiving from… [in this example, Mother Mary].

- Find a sound for the missing quality of trust and make the sound out loud. Use a vowel sound if possible as it increases breathing into the body and as such helps to relax the physical body. Alternatively think of a song that reminds you of this quality of trust and sing the song or listen to it.

- Draw a picture in colour representing the new flow of breath of trust just received from Mother Mary that is now flowing through the body. Place this image next to the first image of the betrayed one.

Quality of trust received from Mother Mary

Step 3: Repeat all of the points in Step 2 but this time using the second image chosen by the client to represent trust. In this case the client has chose their Nana and their drawing was as follows:

Quality of trust received from my Nana

Step 4: Repeat all of the points in Step 2 again but this time using the third image chosen by the client to represent trust. In this case the client chose their dog and the drawing was as follows:

Quality of trust received from my dog

Step 5: Now ask the client to place their hands on the same part of the body where the initial feeling of betrayal was located. Ask them to sense into that part of the body and draw a single large picture showing the flow of energy in that part of the body having now received trust from these three figures including the dog. This is the post-intervention image that represents the transformed image that is a result of the cognitive shift from betrayal to trust.

Post-intervention: the trusting one

Now place the original image on the ground, and the three resources of the images of trust around it. Then place the fifth piece of art, the 'Post-intervention: the trusting one', over the first piece so that the client now has the overall view of the guided imagery transformation.

The completed betrayal to trust sequence

The arrangement of all images is the same as in the preceding two sequences. The client takes a photograph on their phone of this final arrangement, and if they so desire they may take the drawings with them. They place them in a significant place in their home where they can daily renew these images by visualising them and consciously taking a few deep breaths to breathe in these new qualities. It is recommended the client complete this exercise everyday for at least seven days.

Interpretation

The new images provide the client with positive enhancing visualisations to support new positive, cognitive perceptions of themselves. The pre-intervention and post-intervention images illustrate how in the post-intervention the colours lighten, expand and flow, all signs of the breath returning to the part of the body previously contracted by the betrayal. The dark imagery of the pre-intervention with its contracted heart is replaced by imagery that has light colours, expansiveness and is flowing and that represents a new gesture for the client's body that is upright and positive. This means more uprightness, more peace and a new positive cognitive perception.

Comparison of pre- and post-intervention images

CONCLUSION

The four repeatable sequences in this chapter demonstrate clear delineated steps for using guided imagery and breathing to assist in transforming negative cognitive perceptions and experiences into positive cognitive images and positive internal dialogue. These creative CBT sequences provide clear pathways for clients to move from negative, self-defeating cognitive imagery and behaviours to positive imagery. This increases the likelihood that ensuing behaviours will be more positive than prior to the interventions. However, it is important that the client follow through post-session with the positive images they have drawn. They must continue to breathe in the named quality from the named persons for at least the following seven days to consolidate the potential for behavioural changes in line with the new reframed cognitive imagery.

5

SOCIAL SKILLS TRAINING AND BEHAVIOURAL EXPERIMENTS

SOCIAL SKILLS TRAINING

Social skills training is an essential part of CBT, and the use of such skills training has been extensively documented. Some examples include Laugeson and Park (2014) for working with adolescents with autism, Lineham (2015) and Manning and Ridgeway (2016). While modelling and role plays can provide concrete sensory experience for clients to observe and practise improved social skills, other creative therapies also offer a wealth of sensory-based social skills training opportunities that are particularly relevant to children under the age of 12 years.

There is a workbook for teachers to meet the emotional literacy objectives in the school curriculum. It comprises an array of repeatable social skills exercises based in the creative therapies to cultivate self-awareness, self-responsibility, social awareness, responsible decision making and relationship skills (Sherwood 2011). Children learn much better through hands-on experiences rather than through abstract cognitive ideas and words.

In this chapter, several creative therapeutic interventions are outlined that are repeatable, observable and that contribute greatly to the development of better social skills. They provide examples of what can be achieved by these creative approaches to CBT. There are examples drawn from clay therapy, drama therapy and colour therapy.

SPEAKING UP FOR ONESELF: CLAY THERAPY EXERCISE

Many clients with low self-esteem and/or depression have among their cluster of unskilful social behaviours the inability to speak up for who they are. They therefore fail to create opportunities for themselves in complex situations and to represent their points of view. They often feel they are victims or have little control over their destinies. Removing blocks to speaking up for oneself is one of the tasks required to facilitate the reclaiming of a space in which one can start to make one's own decisions and a person can start to feel in control of their life rather than powerless. Clay provides a very concrete observable medium for illustrating the block to speaking up in a very sensory manner, and also gives the client the opportunity to experience bodily the need for a concentrated focus to speak up for oneself in any particular situation.

Materials

- working board about half a metre by half a metre
- a water spray bottle
- an airtight bucket of standard pottery clay in one of the earth hues
- towel for cleaning hands
- three good hand-sized balls of clay
- implements for cutting and carving the clay

Note: Any jewellery, and particularly rings, will need to be removed.

Directions

Step 1: Expressing the shape of the block.

- Ask the client to recall an incident in which they did not speak up and that cost them a feeling of power or that prevented them having input into decisions affecting their life. Draw out the specifics of the situation as much as possible by questioning them about the details and circumstances of the event and of the other persons involved.

- Ask the client to find the part of the body that feels most uncomfortable on recalling the incident.

- Ask the client to place both hands on that part of their body.

- Ask the client to sense how the breath is not moving in that part of the body.

- Ask the client to gesture the shape of the block.

- Ask the client to make the shape of the block in clay.

Step 2: To make an implement to break through the block.

- Ask the client to visualise what implement would be needed to break through the block. Give an example: Is it like an axe, sword, oxyacetylene blowtorch, chainsaw, screwdriver, chisel, shovel or knife?

- Ask the client make the implement in clay.

Step 3: Breaking through the block.

- Ask the client to apply the tool they have made to the block using a sound and gesture of the implement... for example, if it is a hammer, the sound might be *bhh, bhh...* so the client repeats this while banging the block with the hammer that they have made from clay.

- The sound and gesture of the implement is repeated until the client experiences that the block has been broken through and the clay block has been demolished or squashed, or is in pieces from the repetitive action.

- Ask the client to exit or step backwards and make in clay what remains of the block after it has been broken through.

Step 4: Speaking up.

- Ask the client to speak up to the person in the situation and have them speak aloud what they did not say. If necessary, assist them formulate the wording of what they needed to say but did not say before.

- Have the client rehearse this process of speaking up with the counsellor witnessing it, until the client senses the power of speaking up.

This process is illustrated below. The client found the block in their stomach and used a hammer to break it down. They then made a star to represent that they could now speak up because they had broken through the block that was preventing them from standing up for their rights in a particular work situation.

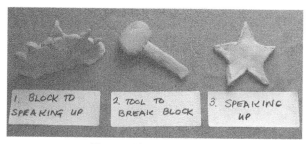

The speaking-up sequence

This process is particularly suitable for children from the age of seven upwards, and with adolescents as well as adults, and can be done singly with a client or in small groups. It is important to ensure that the tool is strong enough to break the block, and it is sometimes useful to spend time exploring the substance the client imagines the block to be composed of. Is it brick, stone, wood or metal? This will affect the fit with the chosen implement. In cases when the block is only partially broken through it is necessary to repeat the application of the implement to the block, until it is completely demolished.

The pre-intervention imprint is the block and usually this is very solid, contracted and represents contracted breathing. The post-intervention is the last piece, the place of speaking up, and generally the clay is now representing more expansive, convex and open shapes, which represent the release of the stress due to the blocked speaking. If this transition does not occur in the shapes of the clay, then the sequence may need to be repeated and a different tool chosen. It is prescribed for the client that each day for seven days following the therapy they speak aloud before a mirror something that they would like to have spoken up about that day, but did not do so.

PROTECTING YOURSELF IN THE FACE OF FEAR: THERAPEUTIC ART EXERCISE

Often it is difficult for clients to understand that their inner thoughts and feelings are realities that may be externalised and observed. They often relate to their inner experiences as though they were in some sort of fog, surrounded by a misty feeling of distress, pain, grief or whatever. This exercise is very simple and is designed to assist the client experience concretely and behaviourally the bodily experience of being attacked through criticism, through other people's physical behaviours towards them or through rejection. Essentially, the client experiences being wounded. They can feel the stress in a particular part of their body when they recount the incident or happenings that have resulted in this feeling. This sequence is particularly powerful in exposing the inner life to those who are cannot articulate it which often include adolescents, resistant clients, reserved clients and males. The aim of the sequence is simply to get the client to gain insight into the reality of their feelings, and to develop an awareness of the ability to protect themselves from particular experiences by creating and using an image and sequence developed from clay therapy.

Materials

- working board about half a metre by half a metre
- a water spray bottle
- an airtight bucket of standard pottery clay in one of the earth hues
- towel for cleaning hands
- three large balls of clay
- sharp object that can be used for cutting or carving the clay

Note: Any jewellery, and particularly rings, will need to be removed.

Directions

Step 1: Capturing the wounded site in the bodily experience of tension.

- The client recalls an experience of feeling emotionally upset or disturbed. Encourage the client to recall the precise details of the situation. Include the physical context, who they were speaking to and any other relevant details. When a complex picture has been visualised by the client, ask the client in which part of the body they feel most uncomfortable when they speak about the experience.

- Ask the client to place their hand on that part of the body.

- Have the client sense into that part of the body.

- Ask the client to sense into the shape of how the breath does not move in this part of the body. Is it lumpy, twisted, tearing, like a rock, a hole…?

- Ask the client to make the shape of how the breath does not move in that part of the body in clay.

This shape represents the stress stored in the client's body through contracted breathing; it is usually contracted, concave and often collapsed in the lines of the clay piece.

Step 2: Capturing the force/attack that creates the wounding.

- Have the client recall the incident again.

- Direct the client to sense again into their body.

- Ask the client to sense the force that creates the wounding.

- Ask them to identify the shape of the force in a very concrete manner. Is it like arrows, a hammer, a vice, a saw, and so on?

- When the client has identified the shape of the force causing the wounding ask the client to make the shape of the force in clay.

- Upon completion, place the force next to the wound. There will be a fit of the shapes, that is, the shape of the wound could have been made by the shape of a force/attack of this nature.

Step 3: Creating a guard to protect the wound from the attack.

- Have the client reflect on the wound and the attack/force that they are experiencing as creating the wound.

- Reflect with the client about possible guards that could be created and placed to protect the wound from the force.

- Ask the client to make the guard in clay.

- Have them place the guard between the wound and the force.

- Enlarge the power of the guard by having the client stand in the gesture of the guard.

- Ask the client to create a sound for the guard and make the sound aloud or choose a song for the guard.

- Ask the client to create a colour for the guard and give the guard a name.

- Ask the client to stand between the wound and the force in the gesture of the guard making the sound of the guard or playing the song that makes them feel protected.

- Ask the client to visualise the guard protecting them on a daily basis, particularly when they feel vulnerable to particular persons or happenings.

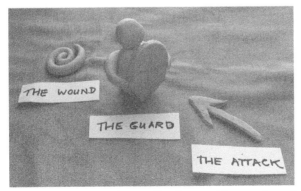

The protective guard between the attacking force and the experienced wound

CREATING AND MAINTAINING BOUNDARIES AND PERSONAL SPACE: DRAMA THERAPY EXERCISE

This sequence drawn from drama therapy is useful for helping clients understand and create effective boundaries in human relationships. Boundaries are essential to avoid aggressive and passive responses and to maintain an assertive or speaking-up position. It is essential with all clients who find that they feel overwhelmed by the demands of others around them, who experience themselves as victims, and who often find it difficult to say no, even in situations that are not in their best interest. Some clients who have poor boundaries respond inappropriately with anger while others collapse inwards and do not protect their best interests. Either response is unskilful, and this exercise is designed to enable both of these types of clients to develop strong boundaries and a clear personal space.

This is an exercise using sound to make audible and more visible how boundaries work. The aim of this exercise is to see which sounds deter people from walking into your space and leave you feeling in command of your own personal space. Many aggressive responses are a result of people feeling invaded in their personal space by other people's words or actions.

Directions

Step 1: Face the client standing about three metres apart.

Step 2: Make the sound '*Oooo…*', or any vowel sound, and ask the client to walk towards you with their eyes closed and stop when they sense that the sound is stopping them getting closer. The client will find that vowel sound does not stop them and they will keep walking up towards the person until they are inside the other person's personal space.

Step 3: Repeat Steps 1 and 2 but this time repeating the consonant *D*: '*D, D, D…*' The client will stop well outside the counsellor's personal space and will experience this as a blocking sound.

Step 4: Repeat this exercise swapping places so that the client experiences the difference between trying to maintain their personal space using *O* versus *D*.

Step 5: Have the client make a protective dome all the way around them as if building it with bricks using the consonant *D*. They need to do this every day for two months. It takes about 30 seconds per day.

In the future in the presence of hostile or unwanted advances, the client repeats '*D, D, D…*' continuously in their mind while visualising the protective dome.

Follow-up

Set up a behavioural activation experiment so that the client can validate that this '*D, D, D…*' works for them in the face of feeling that their personal space is being invaded by unwelcome or hostile persons.

The following case study shows a typical type of behavioural experiment that I would design around this exercise.

> Rebecca is 16 years old, very beautiful and has just obtained a job at the checkout of a major retailer. She has found that men are regularly asking her for her phone number and she feels unable to refuse. After work she is then feeling harassed by unwanted callers trying to arrange dates with her. This is happening at least once a day and sometimes twice a day when she is working at the checkout. Rebecca does not want to give up her job but she wants to feel confident enough to say 'No' when asked for her telephone number.
>
> Rebecca records the number of daily requests and follow-up phone calls that she receives for one week at work when she is on the checkout. The following week she follows the instructions of repeating '*D, D, D…*' aloud in the morning before leaving for work and imaging the protective wall around her. At work she repeats '*D, D, D…*' silently as she serves male customers and visualises the protective wall around her. At the end of the first week, Rebecca's unwanted male advances had dropped from nine per week to two per week. After implementing the boundary strategy for three weeks, she no longer had any unwanted advances while she was working and had not given out her phone number to a single male.
>
> The situations to which this behavioural activation process can be applied are extensive as poor personal boundaries are often a characteristic of many clients presenting in therapy. While weak boundaries are not their only problem, poor boundaries often play

a very significant role in aggravating a wide range of the client's presenting issues.

BEHAVIOURAL EXPERIMENTS

Here the aim is to transform behaviour and feelings into concrete observable actions, which are, of course, one of the great strengths of the creative therapies used in a focused applied manner. When done well, it gives clients concrete tools to apply to their experience in their day-to-day life so that they become aware of behavioural patterns and learn to self-manage their behaviours and consciously move from destructive to constructive behaviours.

SELF-RESOURCING AND SELF-SOOTHING SEQUENCE: CLAY THERAPY

Let us take the example of 'neediness'. Many people have an inability to self-soothe and become fearful and/or irritable if their excessive demands for attention and assistance from those around them are not fulfilled. This has a particularly destructive effect on their interpersonal relationships and in some of the worst cases they become even more needy and isolated as people around them avoid them because of their excessive demands. Such people pressurise and demand from their friends, and acquaintances, time, friendship and help. Begin this process by assisting the client to identify real needs from excessive needs. Assist them to read the body language of people, so they can distinguish when a person is willingly helping them from when a person is finding their demands excessive, and either avoiding them or complying with irritation or annoyance.

This exercise is designed to help the client to self-soothe and self-resource when feeling excessively needy of other people's time and attention and when they have developed an awareness that their demands are being experienced as excessive by the other person's verbal and/or non-verbal cues.

Materials

- working board about half a metre by half a metre

- a water spray bottle

- an airtight bucket of standard pottery clay in one of the earth hues

- towel for cleaning hands

- at least 2 kg of clay

- implements for cutting or carving the clay

Note: Any jewellery, and particularly rings, will need to be removed.

Directions

Step 1: Make in clay the feeling of 'neediness': a shape or gesture that represents this feeling of neediness that drives the behaviour to demand excessive attention from friends and acquaintances.

Step 2: identify the qualities that the client feels are missing in their life that they usually try to obtain from other people that are in excess of what friends and acquaintances are willing to give. A sample selection of such qualities may include warmth, attention, fun, love.

Step 3: The client identifies some archetypal person, place, animal or natural environment that represents each of these qualities. For each quality listed, the client undertakes the following sequence so that the quality is experienced in the body.

- Imagine receiving the quality from the image you have chosen.

- Breathe in the quality as if the air is full of it for at least three deep breaths.

- Visualise a colour for that quality.

- Make the gesture for the quality.[1]

---

1 For example if the quality is love you might have your arms in the gesture of an embrace as you walk around the room. It is very important that the client becomes aware of the different bodily gestures that reflect particular emotional states. They need to sense how the shape of their body changes when they focus upon positive qualities such as love, warmth, joy or nurturance compared with the gesture when they are feeling, unloved, rejected, alone, sad or fearful.

- Make a sound for the particular quality while you walk around the room in the gesture or play a song that represents the quality.

- Make the gesture of the quality in clay.

Step 4: Sculpturing the archetype representing all of these qualities in one piece

- When all the qualities have been made in clay then sense into them all.

- Stand in a gesture that represents the totality of these qualities.

- Make the archetype of these qualities in one large clay piece as a follow-up project at home, school or the counselling session if there is sufficient time.

Self-resourcing and self-soothing sequence

The piece representing all of the qualities in one gesture

Follow-up

Behavioural activation instructions for the client: Take the sculptured qualities home and whenever feeling in need, repeat the process of breathing in the qualities, gesturing them and sounding them. Do this at least daily or whenever the excessively needy feeling arises. Construct a chart showing the number of times friends and acquaintances were requested to help/entertain you before the intervention. Mark on the chart the number of demands made upon friends and acquaintances after the behavioural intervention for one week, two weeks, or three weeks. Show the number of times excessive attention seeking behaviour has been deflected by self-soothing and self-resourcing. If the initial start prior to the behavioural intervention was six times a day, then set a goal to reduce this to three times a day by the end of one week, twice a day by the end of week two and not more than once a day by the end of week three.

This is a powerful resourcing sequence to shape the client's behaviour in the direction of building their sense of power over their life. It can be done with any person aged from six years onwards. It is beneficial for all clients to create each quality in clay because it creates a strong new image that can provide the foundation for behavioural activation practice for the client. On completion of the clay sculpture of the archetype, it is recommended that it be kept and fired if possible. Then the client has a visible reminder of their ability to access their own resources and self-soothe on a daily basis or as required.

PAIN MANAGEMENT SEQUENCE: DRAMA THERAPY EXERCISE

This exercise is useful for assisting clients to contribute in the self-management of pain in some appropriate circumstances.

Materials

- working board about half a metre by half a metre
- a water spray bottle
- an airtight bucket of standard pottery clay in one of the earth hues

- towel for cleaning hands

- at least 2 kg of clay

- implements for cutting or carving the clay

Directions

Step 1: The client develops a rating scale out of 10 to rate the level of their pain.

Step 2: They then sense into the area of pain and how they experience the force of the pain attacking their body. Is it like a stabbing pain, or is it a cutting pain, a tearing pain, a throbbing pain, a burning pain, a gripping pain, a gnawing pain? They make the shape of the pain in clay.

Step 3: The client senses into the quality of the pain and makes the gesture and sound of the pain as they experience it attacking them. They make the shape in clay of the attacking force.

Step 4: They then visualise an image of a shield that they could place between themselves and the pain and using guided imagery they draw or make in clay a guard that could protect them from the force of the pain attacking them. They make the shape of the guard in clay.

Protecting the client from the pain

Step 5: The client with their hands makes the opposite gesture to the force of the pain attacking them and the opposite sound to the attacking sound over the part of the body that is in pain. They repeat the opposite sound and gesture for five minutes. So for example if the attacking pain force is experienced as a stabbing force with the sound '*K, K, K…*' then the client would repeat an opening-up sound and gesture such as '*Arrrh, arrrh*' to deflect the stabbing force in the opposite direction (from a conversation with Yehuda Tagar, author of *Philophonetics*).

After five minutes ask the client to rate the level of experienced pain. Has it declined, remained the same or intensified? In most cases, clients experience a decline in pain. When the pain declines then this behavioural exercise can be added to the client's toolbox of pain management techniques.

Making visible the invisible life of cognitions and feelings is core to these sequences so that clients can readily observe cognitive and affective dynamics in their lives and alter them, so that the behavioural outcomes are more positive and functional in their lives.

MANAGING ANXIETY: BEHAVIOURAL EXPERIMENTAL SEQUENCE

These creative behavioural-based sequences for managing anxiety have been trialled with clients. Clients are asked to rate out of 10 their anxiety on a scale that has been established with them in the initial counselling sessions: say ten is extreme, five is average, and one is very low. The client is then asked to try out each one of the following activities, one at a time when they are feeling anxious for five minutes on each occasion. They rate their anxiety before they commence the exercise and after they complete the exercise, then record the two measures and date them in their therapy logbook. Each of the exercises has anxiety-reduction outcomes for some clients and the purpose of this behavioural experiment is to find out which exercise has maximum effect on reducing anxiety levels for the particular client.

Marching exercise

The client stamps their feet while repeating: 'I am here, I am safe, I am protected' over and over again in rhythm with the stamping feet. Actually marching up and down on the spot will assist the client develop the required rhythm and pressure on their feet.

Squatting exercise

The client repeatedly half-squats to the level where they feel pressure on their ankles while repeating: 'I am here, I am safe, I am protected.' They should do at least ten squats where they can feel pressure on their ankles.

Rolling feet exercise

The client rolls both feet over on their outer edges, so that a pulling sensation is experienced, which makes one become present again, and remains in that position for three minutes while repeating: 'I am here, I am safe, I am protected.'

Running exercise

The client either goes for a run for five minutes or does five minutes running on a treadmill or cross trainer. Based on these results, clients then formulate which assists them most effectively in managing their anxiety.

CONCLUSION

Social skills training and psycho-education are central to counselling today, and these creative approaches to CBT provide a range of concrete mediums to enable new skills to be practised and often made visible and readily observable by the client. They can provide an important adjunct to CBT verbal social skills training processes. In addition, they can be designed to provide behavioural experiments which enable clients to self-validate processes that promote the behavioural changes they desire. In particular, children and adolescents benefit profoundly by the concretisation of social skills while adolescents particularly enjoy behavioural experiments that give them an opportunity to develop their growing need for self-autonomy.

6

COGNITIVE RESTRUCTURING AND REFRAMING

INTRODUCTION

Cognitive restructuring (CR) is an established counselling process of learning to identify, analyse and reject irrational or maladaptive thoughts, which are termed cognitive distortions. Examples of such types of fallacious thinking include intellectualising, all-or-nothing thinking, magical thinking, over-generalisations, catastrophising, labelling, emotional reasoning, 'should' statements, personalisation, jumping to conclusions and operating out of selective negative mental filters (Gladding 2009). These essentially faulty, irrational, misleading and negative mind states create and maintain many mental health problems. Beck (1997) in the 1960s was one of the early therapists to focus on negative thinking patterns, which he identified as a major problem with his work with clients with depression. He termed this process of changing negative thinking patterns into positive rational thinking patterns cognitive restructuring. Albert Ellis (1961) was also an avid proponent of cognitive restructuring in his rational emotive therapy (RET).

The efficacy of cognitive restructuring has been well established by a number of researchers for a range of mental health issues. These include Cooper and Steere (1995) with clients with bulimia; Harvey, Inglis and Espie (2002) with those experiencing insomnia; Hope *et al.* (2010) with clients experiencing social anxiety; and Kanter, Schildcrout and Kohlenberg (2005) and Martin and Dahlen (2005) with clients with depression.

Cognitive restructuring employs many strategies, including thought journalling, guided imagery, cognitive appraisal, cost–benefit analysis, thought analysis, cognitive rehearsal and de-labelling. Cognitive restructuring is therefore very compatible with the creative therapeutic sequences that follow. They are focused upon restructuring the client's cognitive perceptions of their world, from negative disempowering images and thoughts to positive empowering images and thoughts.

GAINING COGNITIVE PERSPECTIVES ON GUILT: THE COMPASSION TRIANGLE

Cognitive restructuring that involves the restructuring of negative automatic thoughts of judgement and self-recrimination into positive thoughts of self-acceptance and understanding is illustrated in the sequence below, which is termed a compassion triangle. It combines a number of creative therapies, including gesture, sound and clay, to facilitate this process of cognitive restructuring at the level of observable behaviour and associated cognitions.

The experience of guilt prevents one from living in the present moment and is maintained by a number of distorted cognitive thinking styles including all-or-nothing thinking, like 'If I'm not perfect, I'm a failure' and over-generalising, 'Because this is wrong, everything I have ever done is also wrong.' Another example is personalisation of events and happenings so that the client engages in self-blame and disqualifies the positives with thinking like 'I have never done anything worthwhile, I am always a failure.' Everything is contaminated by what should have been, what ought to have been done. The client feels trapped between the dominant irrational voice within that condemns them for not living up to certain standards and a submissive but rational voice that understands their difficulties and strengths. The client may alternate from one voice to another within their psyche, or remain stuck on the voice of condemnation and guilt. In either case, there is no rest or inner peace.

The compassion triangle, developed by Tagar (1996), is an effective process for separating out the irrational critic or judge from the compassionate or understanding/rational voice within each of us. This sequence is excellent for working with clients suffering from guilt, self-blame and self-judgement. It illustrates a precise cognitive process for changing the thought patterns that maintain self-condemnation and guilt into self-acceptance.

Materials

- working board about half a metre by half a metre

- a water spray bottle

- an airtight bucket of standard pottery clay in one of the earth hues

- towel for cleaning hands

- at least 2 kg of clay

- implements for cutting or carving the clay

Directions

To begin a compassion triangle, the client needs to recall a specific instance with a specific person in which they feel guilty or a failure and the associated negative self-talk, such as 'I'm bad and unworthy of happiness because I did not help when my mother moved house', 'I'm guilty of not being a good daughter', and such like. The place in which the disturbance/stress is experienced in the client's body is the point of entry into this process.

The points of the triangle represent the two primary cognitive positions that a person who is weighted down with guilt and self-condemnation experiences. They are diagrammatically illustrated below. The client is termed the 'guilty one', and one voice is the 'judge voice' while the other voice is the 'compassionate voice', representing the two cognitive positions that are the options for the client.

Mark this triangle on the floor using cushions or sheets of A4 paper to identify the 'guilty one' and the two positions so that the client can visibly and objectively view the situation in a concrete manner. This enables the client to see more clearly their cognitive options and their choices.

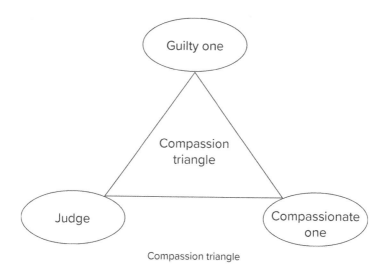

Compassion triangle

1. *The guilty one:* The first position is the 'guilty one' or the part of the cognitive thinking distortion that carries the message of pain and trauma in relation to the recurrent thoughts of guilt and failure. The person who experiences themselves as guilty is caught in a destructive cycle of cognitive thinking that locks them into self-judgement and low self-esteem.

2. *The judge:* The second position in the compassion triangle is the part that reacts to the condemned one with judgement and blame, and creates the cognitive voice position of judgement or the judge. Although unaware, adult clients who have strong cognitive judge voices have usually experienced much judgement in their lives. The judge is always a voice of a significant other or others, a parent, sibling, teacher or other power holder in a child's world that provides the initial imprint for condemnation and judgement. Eventually, after repeated assaults, the child comes to internalise the judge voice that 'I am to blame' and continues as an adult to run this message. The extent of the judgement is measured by the number of judges, their psychic height and the intensity of condemnation in the tone of the client when speaking from the cognitive framework of the judge. The archetypal representation of darkness, destruction, negativity and disempowerment is represented by this position in the cognitive processes.

3. *The compassionate one:* The third position is the part of the client that is capable of compassion and of understanding. It is

the reservoir of the positive self-healing qualities. Here the client can access the qualities needed for self-healing. In this position, all the compassionate voices of understanding that have imprinted on the child's vulnerable psyche are accessible as resources to the adult. Archetypically, this is the position of ultimate goodness and compassion, the place of nourishing and healing resources that can be accessed through positive thinking and imagery creation.

The compassion triangle comprises five steps. The process of this sequence has been adapted for clay therapy by Sherwood from Tagar's original notion (1996) and is described below:

Step 1: The gesture of the guilty/bad one.

The client describes the feeling of guilt and self-condemnation when they recount in detail a particular experience. When they finish, ask the client to sense where in the body they feel the tension when they recall the experience. Then, they draw the shape of how they are not breathing, that is how the tension is stored in their body. Is it like a rock, a ball of string, a knot, a hole, or a twisted rope? This is the place of trauma, the place of guilt, unworthiness, of feeling hopeless and valueless. Ask the client to make in clay the shape of the feeling of being judged as guilty.

The guilty one

This is the position of trauma of the condemned/guilty one, and is marked on the ground with a label THE GUILTY ONE and the clay piece is placed on this A4 paper. This enables the client to view the trauma from a distance. Rate the feelings of badness/guilt out of ten from a scale created by therapist and client. For example, 10 might be extremely guilty, and 0 not guilty at all and 5 half guilty. This is the time to reflect on the automatic thoughts that drive and maintain the feeling of guilt.

Step 2: Developing insight into the judge position.

Here the counsellor asks the client to stand in the position of the voice of condemnation and judgement and while in this position to sense the voice of anger, judgement and condemnation directed at the guilty one. Have the client speak aloud the negative condemning thoughts to the condemned guilty one. Externalise these cognitive distortions by speaking them aloud from the judge voice: 'You are bad because you have not fulfilled your responsibilities as a husband', 'You have no right to leave the marriage for any reason because marriage is forever', 'Society will reject you because you have failed to be a good person', and other such cognitive distortions.

Upon completion of speaking out the voice of the judge, who represents all of these cognitive distortions and judgements directed against the client, ask the client to look behind their back and to tell you who they see standing there joining in the condemnation. There will usually be a group of key judges in their life: a parent, sibling, teacher. Ask the client how tall are the judges. The number of judges and their height indicates the extent of the self-condemnation and guilt. A large number of tall judges will usually suggest that a number of compassion triangles will be needed. Ask the client to gesture and make in clay this judge voice. Bring to the client's awareness the cognitive distortions underlying this negative voice, including generalisations, all-or-nothing thinking, personalisation and disqualifying the positive, to name a few of the possibilities. At this point, the client makes the judge in clay representing all of these negative messages directed towards the guilty one. The clay judge is then placed on an A4 sheet labelled THE JUDGE VOICE, arranged to face towards the guilty one.

The judge voice and the guilty one

Step 3: Understanding the compassionate voice and the positive voice of reasonable logical cognitive thinking.

Now ask the client to speak from the voice of understanding, which is the voice of compassionate understanding that embraces human limitations, and understands human weaknesses with explanation and rationality rather than condemnation. Sometimes the client cannot access this voice within themselves because it has been so extinguished in their life. Then it is essential to stop the process and go and find a compassionate figure in their life. One needs only to find one voice, a teacher, a friend, a significant adult who understood and valued the client. If one cannot be found then the client needs to access an archetypal resource such as Mother Teresa, Nelson Mandela, Kannon, Krishna, Jesus or Mother Mary from whom they can receive compassionate understanding and who can speak to the client from their position of understanding and acceptance of their behaviour.

Begin this section with the client speaking from the understanding position and facing the guilty one while they are doing this: 'I understand why you did it. It was because [insert the reasons of the particular client case]. This does not make you a bad person…' When the client has completed speaking, the counsellor asks the client to turn around and look at who stands behind them. The height and the number of persons standing here is also very important as it indicates the client's compassionate and understanding resources. This process inevitably takes the client to the position of compassion and understanding towards self and creates a space for a rational and balanced view of themselves. Clients then gesture and make in clay the experience of understanding and acceptance of their limitations, which is a part of being a human being.

This is the time to discuss and restructure the client's cognitions about their behaviour so that they are now positive, self-accepting and self-empowering. They now understand how the judge position was characterised by faulty logic. Now ask the client to make the gesture in clay of self-acceptance and place this on a third sheet of paper labelled THE COMPASSIONATE VOICE.

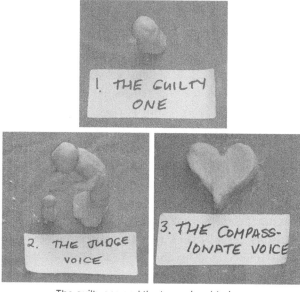

The guilty one and the two voices/choices

Step 4: The empowerment sequence – dealing with the judge.

The client now enters back into the gesture of the guilty/condemned one to find out how the experience of the judge's condemnation is attacking them. Is it like a stab from a knife, a punch, a kick, a slap, being winded, a sword in their heart? Once they have identified the force of the attack, using gesture and sound, encourage the client to remove the force. If it is a knife or a sword, pull it out in gesture and throw it out the window with an appropriate sound. While reversing the force/attack and throwing it away from the body and out the window encourage the client to breathe deeply, for example from a narrow '*nnn*' to an expanded out-breath like '*Uuuuhh…*'. It is essential that the client breathes deeply at least three times after removing the force or experience of the attack of the judgement. In the case of a slap or punch, push it away.

Once completed, ask the client to turn around and sense how many judge voices are still present and how high they are. Depending on the change from the original profile of the judges, one can ascertain what shift has been made in the client's thinking. If the cognitive skills training has been successful and the guided imagery through the clay work process has been effective, one will expect the number and sizes of judge voices to have diminished at this point in the sequence.

Depending on the remaining height of the judges and their relative strength, the counsellor can predict what future work needs to be done around the issue. In some cases, the judges will disappear entirely.

Step 5: Resourcing and invoking – accessing the powerful compassionate resources.

The session should always conclude with revisiting the compassionate rational voices and enlarging them again. Now make the image in the last piece of clay of self-acceptance. Encourage the client to photograph their whole sequence as illustrated below so they can focus upon the task clearly post session as they revise the compassionate voice position of self-acceptance and forgiveness.

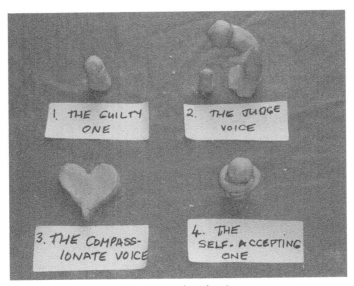

The compassion triangle

At the end of the session, the compassionate voices should be taller, larger and more accessible to the client. For at least two weeks, the client needs to re-run a positive voice daily and dismiss any recurrence of the judge voices with the positive affirmation.

THERAPEUTIC ART EXERCISE FOR RESTRUCTURING: SELF-ESTEEM TREES

Low self-esteem children and adults who are underachievers often hold deeply sabotaging beliefs about themselves, and are highly prone to irrational, negative cognitive patterns. Shame is deeply rooted at the core of the individual's self-esteem. It consists of messages from adults that devalue the child in such profound ways that, as an adult, these devaluing toxic statements cripple the individual's ability to manifest their potential. Very often at the core of the devaluing self-perception are body-shame-based messages, such as 'I am too fat', 'I am dirty', 'I smell', 'I am ugly'. Added to this are a string of messages about the absence of cognitive and social abilities, such as 'I am worthless', 'I am stupid', 'I am hopeless', 'I am incompetent', 'I am a burden on others', 'I am lazy', 'I am uncouth'. The adult client suffering shame often feels that something is deeply wrong with themselves, despite objective assessments to the contrary from other people. In fact, core to low self-esteem are major cognitive distortions, including all-or-nothing thinking, over-generalising, disqualifying the positive, magnification, emotional reasoning and personalisation.

Materials

- A set of brightly coloured crayons in a range of colours
- 2 sheets of A4 paper
- a black marker pen

Directions

The client who wishes to improve their self-esteem begins by creating a low self-esteem or shame tree, each root representing one of the core toxic cognitive messages of failure or devaluation that the client believes. This is illustrated below:

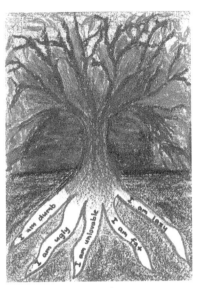

Low self-esteem/shame tree

A self-esteem tree is then created that contains the same amount of roots as the toxic tree but with each root representing the positive alternative messages that are a result of the cognitive restructuring. These trees become the diagnostic counselling plan for the number of counselling sessions and types of interventions required.

Self-esteem tree

Common core messages in the self-esteem tree that are sabotaged by negative cognitive worldviews are:

I am intelligent

I am good looking

I can accomplish things

I am attractive

I am knowledgeable

I am competent

I work well

I am lovable

I am useful

I am healthy

Each of the core messages in the self-esteem tree becomes the cognitive restructuring goal for the therapy session. So for example, the 'I am useless' low self-esteem message is exposed as all-or-nothing thinking, over-generalising, magnification and personalisation to the client; and the alternative message, the new positive esteem building message, in this case 'I can accomplish things', replaces it. The concretisation of this positive worldview occurs post session through exercises to affirm this reality, and on occasions a behavioural experiment, so that the client can deeply understand how replacing negative, distorted worldviews with positive, rational worldviews leads them to feel better about themselves.

A therapy session is devoted to each low self-esteem message initially identified in session one until all the cognitive thinking distortions that underlie the low self-esteem tree have been explored and replaced with positive rational cognitive messages that support the client's well-being and happiness.

SAND TRAY EXERCISE FOR CLEARING COGNITIVE DISTORTIONS THAT UNDERLIE SELF-HARM (CUTTING)

Although some adolescents talk a great deal about their cutting escapades to each other, photograph it and circulate it via their mobile phones, they do not have an in-depth understanding about what drives the process, or its costs, or about interventions that they could make to prevent themselves engaging in the process. This exercise is directed at exposing the negative cognitive distortions that underlie self-harm.

Materials

- sand tray half full with yellow/white/golden clean sand, a rectangular box (with a blue base to represent water, if possible) approximately 75 cm by 55 cm and 15 cm high

- sand tray pieces – at least 50 are recommended to start your collection

Sand tray pieces should include some of the following categories of toys to represent good and bad feelings:

- *Earth* – Volcanoes, gems, crystals, rocks, mountains, waterfalls

- *Plant* – Forests, trees, roses, flowers, fruits, cactus, nuts, seeds

- *Animal* – Tigers, lions, snakes, birds, butterflies, spiders, dinosaurs, sharks, dolphins, dogs, cats, lizards, elephants, monkeys, rabbits, frogs, fish, eagles, bees, bugs, horses, sheep, giraffes, butterflies, birds, feathers

- *Human* – Children, babies, adults (male and female), soldiers, warriors, old and young persons, fat and thin people, racially diverse people, clowns, sad and happy persons, mothers, fathers, kings, queens

- *Archetypal* – Wizards, fairies, angels, Buddha, Jesus, Mary, cross, star, crescent, magic wand, baddies, goodies

- *Mechanical and objects* – Cars, bridges, houses, buildings, castle, fences, boats, planes, containers, food, mirrors, beds, bikes, containers, boxes, clocks, helicopters, jewellery, money, road, sword, gun, eggs.

Directions

Step 1: Ask the client to choose a piece to represent their feelings when they have the first thoughts about wanting to cut (e.g. 'I am bad and a failure because I failed the maths test today') and to place it in the sand tray.

- Then ask the client to choose a piece for the sand tray that represents how they feel and think when they are preparing to cut (e.g. 'I am hopeless and my father will be angry with me so I feel anxious').

- The client chooses a piece that represents how they feel at the moment of cutting (e.g. 'I am powerful, I have control over my life').

- The client chooses a piece that represents how they feel immediately after cutting (e.g. 'I am relieved and feel calm').

- The client chooses a piece to represent how they feel in the longer term after cutting (e.g. 'I am bad, I feel ashamed').

Cutting sequence

Step 2: Discuss the feelings and thoughts at each of the points above. Work with the presenting trigger and the thoughts at each stage to reveal cognitive distortions and to provide the client with alternative cognitive thinking patterns, which cognitively reframe their experiences into a rational, positive and proactive way of thinking.

Step 3: Ask the client to select additional pieces that represent qualities that could provide sufficient support to the unhappy powerless one and the anxious one, so that they would not need to progress to the powerful cutting one but could go directly to the calm relaxed one.

Step 4: Discuss the implications of this for their lives, and alter the sand tray to reflect these new possibilities while affirming the new cognitive thinking patterns. Photograph the sand tray containing these new possibilities and give a copy to the client.

Follow up with the client the identified new qualities that need to come into their life for them not to need to progress to cutting in order to feel powerful and in control of their life. This will involve a number of internal changes for the client's thinking life as well as external changes such as networking, support mentoring, establishing new opportunities in social, sporting or educational contexts, depending on the client's identified needs and interests.

CONCLUSION

In summary, there are several creative therapeutic exercises, of which I have just identified a few, that could assist in revealing cognitive distortions to clients in a very concrete observable way and that can support clients to move forward and reframe their experiences in a cognitively rational and positive manner.

7

EXPOSURE AND DESENSITISATION

INTRODUCTION

Systematic desensitisation, or graduated exposure therapy, was developed by Wolpe (1958) and is used primarily to overcome phobias and anxiety disorders (Dubord 2011). Wolpe noticed that animals could overcome their fears through gradual and systematic exposure to a frightening stimulus. The process of systematic desensitisation aims to reduce the level of fear gradually by pairing fear with a desirable or relaxing stimulus. This is based upon the notion that a client cannot be fearful and relaxed at the same time. If the paired relaxing stimulus is strong enough, it will enable to client to overcome the fear at that level.

The first part of systematic desensitisation constructs an anxiety-inducing stimulus hierarchy that is paired with a hierarchy of desirable and relaxing stimuli. Essentially, the individual learns how to focus their mind and body on the relaxing stimuli instead of the paired anxiety stimuli, to reduce their level of response to the anxiety stimuli (Agras *et al.* 1971). Efficacy studies have shown this to be a particularly effective treatment for phobias and anxiety (Austin and Patridge1995; Deffenbacher and Hazaleus 1985).

Flooding, developed by Stampfl (1967, cited in Dubord 2011), although initially not as comfortable for the client, is another technique used to desensitise clients' suffering for particular anxieties and phobias. Sometimes referred to as exposure therapy, it exposes the client to the feared object (either in reality or by virtual reality) for such a prolonged period of time that the client's fear response is exhausted. Then the client learns to apply relaxation techniques to replace the fear in face of the feared object.

In this chapter four sequences are presented based on creative therapies that expose the client to the aversive stimuli but then provide repeatable sequential steps for reducing the fear or aversive response that has brought the client to therapy. In addition, there is a brief sequence especially designed for children under ten years.

ENTER–EXIT–BEHOLD SEQUENCE

This sequence is drawn from drama therapy and uses staging to assist the client to manage and recover from their fear and anxiety.

The 'enter–exit–behold' sequence was initially developed by Tagar (1996) and later modified by Sherwood (2004) to become a process for tracking the breath in the body so as to ascertain the location of fear and its management. Through this process, the client can go to the site of their deepest fears, but rather than remain overwhelmed by them and then fall back into some intrusive repetitive stress state, the client can literally step backwards out of the fear and observe their fear from a distance. They are able then to cultivate insight around the fear and transform it. Here the client is capable of beholding the traumatic experience, with all their adult resources mobilised to bring about its release, without remaining flooded by it. The client thus has control over the balance between being flooded by the fear and standing in a calm position and observing the fear.

Materials

- a set of crayons of at least 12 colours
- 4–6 sheets of A4 paper

Directions

Step 1: The client first senses the part of the body where they feel the breath is constricted or tense when they think about their fear. The client places their hand on that part of the body to help track the experience.

- The client then literally steps forward into the imagined part of the body in which they can sense the tension/fear. This is called 'enter'. Here the client is asked to sense the shape of how they are not breathing.

- The client is then asked to literally step backwards and draw the shape of how the energy or breath is constricted in that part of the body. Is it like a tight ball, a flattened piece of wood, a twisted cord, and so on?

Step 2: The client is then asked to step forward and enter the drawn shape by fitting their whole body into the shape. The client then contracts their whole body into the gesture of how they have constricted their breathing. They may be twisted into a gesture of a knot or a tight ball, or another type of compacted gesture. The client chooses the gesture entirely themselves based on their drawing of the constriction in their breathing.

- The client remains in this position that will evoke their fear and memories associated with it.

- From this position, the client re-experiences the active dynamics of the trauma from the inside. The client is not left in this position to experience the terror, pain or fear any longer than is necessary to obtain a snapshot of what is going on. As soon as the client chooses, they can 'exit' the position by standing upwards and stepping backwards. If they are very 'in' and in considerable fear, they may need to step backwards three or four times. With each step backwards, they shake their hands vigorously as if shaking off the experience of fear. 'Exit' means literally physically getting out of the gesture completely, by taking a step backwards and shaking it off by shaking one's hands and arms as if to throw off the sensed experience.

Step 3: The client is asked to move to another physical position in the room that is uncontaminated by the painful experience. The client now beholds the trauma causing the fear from the 'exited' position. It is as if they are outside of the trauma/fear and have a strategic distance from which to observe. Yehuda Tagar, author of *Philophonetics*, described this position to me as the 'verandah' or the place of observation where the client can now see the trauma but feel that they can control their level of fear in relation to it. The client beholds the dynamics involved as an outside observer. This is the act of 'beholding', where the client is getting a clear picture of what is driving the fear that they have just experienced in bodily form. The client is able to share this with the counsellor and identify what they need to do next to continue to reduce the fear.

This technique works effectively to enable the client to uncover the fear dynamics without risk of being flooded and caught back inside the fear that the client has so long been defending against or avoiding. Through this process, the client can go into the site of their fear, but rather than be overwhelmed and fall back into some intrusive stress state, the client can behold the experience and gain a strategic depth with which to manage and transform the trauma. This sequence has been used extensively for work with sexual abuse survivors (as documented by Sherwood 2000b). *It is very effective but not recommended to be used by inexperienced therapists or therapists without training in the technique.*

This process enables the client to enter the inner pattern of experience, then to formally exit it, and finally to proceed to a safe place to behold the dynamic of suffering and to gain the necessary information about the experience to design the healing process. The exit process prevents what is uncovered from flooding the client, or exposing the client's vulnerability in a traumatic way, so that the client moves into an intrusive stress phase. The major contribution of this sequence is towards facilitating a middle position between flooding and emotional detachment. This is described in detail by Sherwood (2000a) in an article on working effectively with sexual abuse survivors.

Very occasionally, the client goes very deeply into the experience and becomes flooded, and even when the client steps backwards they still remain in the experience. Yehuda Tagar has developed a variation of the exit sequence called 'Bamboo' to enable the client to keep exiting by repeating the exiting sequence. This is documented in detail in Chapter 8 under relapse prevention strategies.

CUTTING RECOVERY SEQUENCE

It is essential that the individual develops a very clear picture of the bodily drivers of their cutting. The fear and experience of agitation and powerlessness is not just in their head. This sequence assists the client engaged in cutting to understand and clear the fear and powerlessness that drives the self-harming. Repeated trialling of this exercise has demonstrated that adolescents usually cut themselves following feelings of fear or anxiety. This exercise is intended to provide an alternative process to cutting for dealing with this.

Materials

- oil crayons
- 4 A3 sheets of white drawing paper

Directions

Step 1

- Take a step forward into the part of the body where you feel the fear and powerlessness before you cut.
- Step backwards and draw the shape of how the fear/energy is trapped there. Is it like a rock, a ball of string, etc.?

Step 2

- Step into the shape you have drawn and sense how the fear is attacking you. Is it like an arrow, a punch, etc.?
- Make the gesture of the fear attacking you on a cushion.
- Find the sound of the gesture of the fear. Is it like a punch '*bbb*' or a knife '*kkk*' or a squeezing '*nnn*' sound, or some other sound?

Step 3

- The counsellor makes the sound at the client, which at first is done very quietly and standing some distance from the client.
- If the sound is correct, the client will have an aversive reaction to the sound.
- Encourage the client to block the sound with a loud '*ggg*', '*bbb*' or '*ddd*', depending on which works best for the client while raising their hands in a blocking gesture. Gradually increase the

aversive sound as the client demonstrates that they can block the sound with a '*ggg*', '*bbb*' or '*ddd*'.

- Stop when the aversive sound the counsellor is imitating no longer troubles the client.

Step 4

- The client will now feel stronger and will no longer respond with aversion to the original sound of the force.

- The client should then practice daily for seven days saying out loud the sound that they found protective and successful in blocking the aversive sound, namely the repeated *g*, *b* or *d*. These are strong sounds and the client can use them to create a block against any fear should it recur. The blocking sound should be practised out loud daily for 30 seconds, or in one's mind only in the face of fear in the presence of other people.

This exercise is very useful in empowering an adolescent to overcome their fear and powerlessness by using methods other than cutting. It can be repeated for each different trigger of fear that the adolescent experiences. When the triggers have been dealt with in this way, the cutting will generally reduce and sometimes cease.

This sequence requires formal training to be effected safely and effectively by a therapist.

DEPRESSION RECOVERY SEQUENCE

This sequence drawn from art therapy exposes the client to their depression then provides a clear sequential pathway of steps to enable the client to become desensitised to the depression experience, which otherwise can become an entrenched long-term lifestyle thinking pattern. It could also be said that this exercise reframes the experience using imagery suggestions.

Materials

- A4 paper

- oil crayons or acrylic paints (depending on the client's preference)

Directions

Step 1: Ask the client to sense where in their body they feel the fear of being stuck in depression for the long term and ask them to sense the colours and images of this experience, and paint or draw them on an A4 sheet of paper.

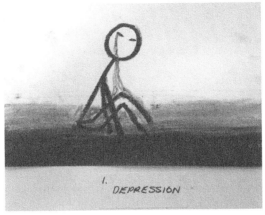

The fear of life-long depression

Step 2: Ask the client to paint or draw the slide into depression by capturing the feeling prior to being so depressed.

The slide into depression

Step 3: Ask the client to name a quality they need to counter the fear of life-long depression. Have them draw or paint something representing this image of the missing quality, and then encourage them to breathe it in deeply for at least two minutes.

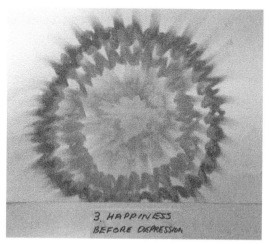

Happiness – the missing quality lost by the depression

Step 4: Place this drawing next to the drawing/painting of the fear of life-long depression, and ask the client to visualise how this quality helps them move out of depression and move on the upward curve back to happiness.

This final drawing/painting represents the movement out of long-term depression. Then ask the client to paint how, after receiving the missing quality and breathing it in, they now feel differently.

Recovering from depression

As a follow-up to these drawings, ask the client daily to imagine burning up their image of the fear of long-term depression, and replace that image with the image of returning to a positive healthy space in their lives. This is represented in image four which the client should be advised to place in a highly visible place in their home where they will see it daily. They then imagine breathing in the missing qualities required to restore their happiness on a daily basis, as they visualise their recovery from depression. I prescribe this follow-up activity for 21 days.

The completed recovering from depression sequence looks like this:

The recovery from depression sequence

FEAR OF ABANDONMENT RELIEF SEQUENCE

This sequence is used to facilitate client recovery and again uses a gradual desensitisation process combined with guided imagery.

Directions

Step 1: Allow the client to feel the fear of abandonment in their body and sense into the feelings that arise in them of hopelessness or despair (or any other feelings named by the client). Ask the client to gesture this fear of abandonment and enlarge it until it reaches the maximum capacity. If necessary clients can lie on the floor, curl up under a table, or do whatever it is that represents the gesture of abandonment.

Step 2: From this position, ask the client to visualise the quality that they need to relieve their fear of abandonment and give them the feeling of safety and connectedness. Ask the client to select the image of a person, animal or place that gives them the feeling of connectedness and comfort. Here again the resource folders mentioned earlier in Chapter 4, will assist clients who have difficulty thinking of a positive image.

Step 3: Take the client through a guided relaxation using the image of comfort and connectedness selected by the client. Have them slowly breathe in the quality of connectedness and comfort… Start with feeling it come into their heart and then from there feel it gradually move through their torso, head, arms legs and to the tips of the fingers and toes. Do this guided relaxation using the client's chosen image for at least 15–20 minutes. Instruct the client that, as they breathe in this new quality of connectedness and warmth they can change their bodily gesture to represent this newfound comfort. They should change the gesture gradually, as the guided relaxation sequence develops.

Step 4: Eventually ask the client to stand in the new gesture of feeling connectedness and comfort that they are now breathing through their whole body. Ask the client to walk around the room in this gesture of recovery. Finally, ask the client to draw or paint the energy of the feeling of connectedness and comfort.

Step 5: Instruct the client to follow up post session by breathing in this quality every day for seven days particularly when they are feeling fear of being abandoned. In the follow-up conversation, explore with the client social, educational or personal activities, sporting or otherwise, that they could engage in that would also give them a sense of connectedness and comfort.

ENLARGING THE LIGHT EXERCISE

This is a simple therapeutic art exercise used for young children to desensitise them to trauma. It can be used whenever a young child is experiencing fear and anxiety.

Materials

- a set of crayons of at least 12 colours
- 2 sheets of A3 paper

Directions

Step 1: Ask the child to draw the colours of the feeling when they have to face their fear, whatever it may be; say, going to a dentist, going to a hospital, going to school. Look closely at the child's drawing and look for the light colour. Usually yellow is first choice followed by light blues or greens. Avoid reds, oranges, browns and dark blues in the drawing. Ask the child to imagine stepping into the yellow and draw a picture of what they see inside the little yellow stripe, line, speck, etc. in the original painting/drawing.

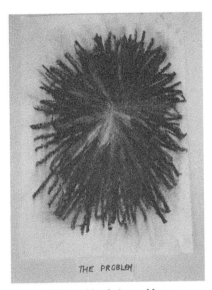

THE PROBLEM

'The problem' place of fear

Step 2: The second picture will represent the place of positive experience. Here the child is encouraged after completing this picture to imagine disappearing into this place when they start to feel fearful. Therefore, they imagine (e.g. when they are sitting in the dentist's chair, disappearing into the beautiful place that they have drawn that is a place of happiness. They are also asked to do this exercise daily when they wake as well in order to become familiar with this place of beauty, happiness and safety, so that when they are in a fearful situation it comes to them easily. This is usually done daily for 14 days.

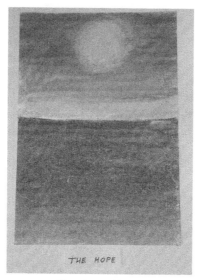

THE HOPE

The place of hope

CONCLUSION

This chapter illustrates how creative approaches to CBT can be used for desensitisation of negative and fearful experiences for clients. Although somewhat different to paired stimuli desensitisation processes, clients reach the goal of desensitisation and increased control over their fear and anxiety responses. This produces more functional behaviours in clients. They become more able to deal with these aversive stimuli in their lives and become more able to enjoy their lives.

8

RELAPSE PREVENTION AND REINFORCERS

INTRODUCTION

Relapse prevention is a central concern of therapists, as new behaviours or skills acquired in the therapy session must be anchored in the individual's life on a daily basis. This takes time, energy, commitment and the establishment of new behavioural routines, both personally and socially. Relapsing into pre-therapy dysfunctional behaviours is a likely outcome for most clients, so it is essential that strategies are developed to assist clients manage or avoid relapses. Much has been documented about relapse prevention in relation to addiction, particularly alcohol (e.g. Witkiewitz and Marlatt 2004).

Relapses for any one individual are determined by a range of interpersonal and intrapersonal factors as well as the socio-economic context in which the individual lives. These include the motivation of the individual to maintain the changed behaviour, and the support available from significant family and social networks to maintain the changed behaviour. The proximity of factors such as freely available alcohol or other addictive substances, peers who are also self-harming, and freely available internet porn and other negative de-motivating sites, may undermine the individual's new behaviours. In addition, poor physical health, socio-economic stressors including low income, overcrowding, homelessness and unemployment may also contribute towards an individual's vulnerability to relapse.

Larimer, Palmer and Marlatt (1999) document a cognitive behavioural model of relapse prevention. This model incorporates many intervention strategies that allow therapist and client to systematically manage the relapse process. Specific interventions include identifying high-risk situations, enhancing the client's skills for coping with those situations, increasing the client's self-efficacy, and managing lapses. Global strategies include assisting the client to develop a healthy lifestyle and employing road maps of the relapse process that alert the client to the signposts of the relapse journey and that help to create potential stopping points in that decline.

Rhythmical and repetitive repetition of appropriate creative therapeutic exercises

In all the creative CBT intervention sequences described in this book, follow-up repetition of the desired behaviour or cognitive restructuring is recommended usually for seven days and sometimes for 14 or 21 days in order to minimise relapse. The 'Grief and loss' sequence (Chapter 4) and the 'Recovery from depression' sequence (Chapter 7), for example, are repeated for 21 days. The 'Enlarging the light' sequence (Chapter 7) is usually completed over a 14-day period, and a seven-day period is prescribed for the 'Speaking-up' sequence (Chapter 5), and the 'Betrayal to trust' and 'Despair to hope' sequences (both Chapter 4). These sequences are designed to support desired inter-session behavioural changes and the efficacy of the interventions is assessed at each follow-up session. They are designed to incorporate relapse prevention and reinforcers specifically in each sequence and this has been indicated within the sequences.

However, there are three relapse prevention strategies that are applied across all of the sequences aimed at behavioural change (as opposed to diagnostic sequences). These three universal relapse prevention strategies are: Exiting, Enlivening and Invoking.

EXITING SEQUENCE 'BAMBOO'

This exercise is called 'Exiting' because it enables the client to literally step out of fear, anger, distress and repetitive dysfunctional thoughts. It was developed by Tagar (1996). It provides very effective management of a range of negative emotions, including fear, anger, flooding, hysteria, repetitive intrusive negative thoughts or images, anxiety, panic, grief and despair. It is a very effective relapse prevention strategy, and it was developed from drama therapy.

The client can be fully exited by undertaking the following simple but effective 'exiting' process.

Directions

Step 1: The client first becomes aware that they are feeling one of the above listed negative cognitions or responses and they sense where in the body it feels to be primarily located. It is located in the place of tension or stress in the body that the client experiences as they dwell on the cognition or experience. This is the place of contracted breathing.

Step 2: The client then:

- places their hands on the part of the body where they feel the identified stress

- collects the stress with both hands literally into a ball shape

- throws away the ball shaped collection of stress out a window while expelling their breath with a loud, 'g', 'uuh', 'd', or similar explosive sound

- steps backwards and stamps their feet loudly and firmly as if marching

- shakes their hands vigorously as if shaking off the bodily stress.

Repeat Step 2 three to six times until the client experiences themselves as no longer feeling the initial stressor whether behavioural, cognitive or emotional.

This sequence was also named 'Bamboo' because it repeats itself several times, just as a bamboo stalk is made up of what appear to be repetitive segments of growth. It is the single most effective relapse prevention sequence, and if clients do it every day as part of a de-stressing relaxing routine it will greatly assist in preventing relapses. It works well in relieving accumulated stress from daily activities and in restoring the breathing. Its use for assisting nurses working with burnout stress has been documented by Sherwood and Tagar (2000a, 2000b).

ENLIVENING SEQUENCE

Enlivening is also an exercise developed by Tagar (1996) to assist clients in becoming present to the present moment by restoring the flow of breathing in the body. There is a direct correlation between bodily movement and breathing more fully into the body. With deeper breathing comes relaxation, increased awareness and concentration in the present moment. A person can then act from a more aware and insightful position and so make skilful choices that deflect dysfunctional behaviours, unskilful cognitions and emotional responses from manifesting.

Directions

This exercise involves the client standing up and slowly moving their body through a series of easy flowing movements that bring them into the present moment. It starts with swaying back and forth for several minutes, followed by stretching back and forth, expanding and contracting the arms back and forth, swinging back and forth and engaging the whole body in this movement. Other bodily movement rhythms and gestures can be added. The pace gradually increases until the client feels their breath is now flowing freely and without any restrictions throughout their body.

The exercise creates a clear space for the client to make skilful and productive decisions for their life. It is recommended that clients also repeat this daily as overall well-being maintenance, as well as at moments when there are triggers that promote relapse behaviours.

INVOKING SEQUENCE

Cognitive and emotive experiences of abandonment, despair, hopelessness, grief, aloneness, weakness and coldness, and absence of love, joy, light, and warmth, tend to surface at moments in the client's life depending on trigger events around them. They leave the client feeling vulnerable, stressed and susceptible to relapse. The process of 'invoking' mobilises the client's positive strengthening and empowering resources in moments of need. This sequence transforms these patterns of depletion into life-giving patterns of joy, hope, promise, warmth, love and celebration.

Directions

This invoking sequence begins with the question: What is the missing quality that you need to recover your strength [or joy, hope, love, connectedness, power, self-worth, or whatever the client needs in the present moment]? Once the missing quality is named, then the client is taken through the following steps to cognitively reframe the experience as positive rather than negative.

- Where in the body do you experience the missing quality? Place your hand on that part of your body.

- Invoke someone spiritual or human, living or dead, animal or being who represents the missing quality and has an abundance of it.

- Imagine receiving this missing quality from them as it rains down upon you.

- Breathe in the missing quality to that part of your body, then let the quality flow throughout your whole body.

- Colour your breath the colour of the missing quality and continue to breathe it in for five minutes.

- Stand in the quality and move with your body around the room in the gesture of having received this missing quality.

- Find a sound or a song for the missing quality and make the sound out loud or sing the song.

- Draw or paint a picture in colour of the flow of the energy of the missing quality or make something in clay to represent the missing quality.

Repeat this exercise as required throughout the day.

In addition to the above generic sequences used to manage and curtail relapses during the inter-session period, there are specific directions to clients based on the presenting issue that assist clients create positive interpersonal and intrapersonal cognitive reminders. These assist them to recognise vulnerabilities and to manage them skilfully.

CONCLUSION

With these relapse prevention sequences of exiting, enlivening and invoking, the creative sequences for CBT practitioners as illustrated in Chapters 2 to 7 provide lucid, repeatable sequences for diagnostic purposes as well as for developing desired behavioural and cognitive changes. Sequences like grounding and anger transformation illustrate how using creative sequences develops self-regulation in clients. Guided imagery work is particularly suitable for creative CBT sequences like grief and loss recovery, and recovery from despair and betrayal as well as self-forgiveness. Social skills training can be achieved by creative CBT sequences such as speaking up, establishing clear boundaries and personal space. Behavioural experiments can be established using creative CBT sequences such as the pain management sequence, and the reducing stress and anxiety sequences. Creative CBT sequences are particularly useful to facilitate cognitive restructuring, including the cutting sequence, the self-esteem building sequence and the compassion triangle. Desensitisation and exposure goals are achieved through creative CBT sequences like the fear sequence, the depression recovery sequence, and the enlarging the light sequence.

All these creative CBT sequences support verbal cognitive behavioural therapy goals and so can become an important adjunct to other verbal strategies and exercises used in CBT. They will provide particularly essential adjuncts for therapists working with children, adolescents, resistant or challenging clients and clients who have low levels of verbal skills or who are unwilling to talk freely or easily. These creative approaches to CBT also engage regular clients in a therapy that is personalised, engaging and motivating. Such creative therapy interventions within CBT offer new opportunities to engage clients and to develop and expand the possibilities of techniques and tools in the therapeutic process.

References

Agras, W., Leitenberg, H., Barlow, D., Curtis, N. and Edwards, J.A. (1971) 'Relaxation in systematic desensitisation.' *Archives of General Psychiatry 25*, 6, 511–514. doi:10.1001/archpsyc.1971.01750180031005

Austin, J. and Partridge, E. (1995) 'Prevent school failure: Treat test anxiety.' *Preventing School Failure 40*, 1, 10–14.

Beck, A. (1997) 'The past and the future of cognitive therapy.' *Journal of Psychotherapy Practice and Research 6*, 276–284.

Bell, A. (2016, 28 September) 'What is self-regulation and why is it so important?' [Blog post]. Retrieved 26 January 2018 from www.goodtherapy.org/blog/what-is-self-regulation-why-is-it-so-important-0928165

Bergland (2014, 1 January) 'Researchers map body areas linked to specific emotions.' *Psychology Today* Retrieved 12 January 2018 from www.psychologytoday.com/blog/the-athletes-way/201401/researchers-map-body-areas-linked-specific-emotions

Cooper, P.J. and Steere J. (1995) 'A comparison of two psychological treatments for bulimia nervosa: Implications for models of maintenance.' *Behaviour Research and Therapy 33*, 875–885. doi:10.1016/0005-7967(95)00033-t

Cunningham, L. (2010) *The Mandala Book: Patterns of the Universe.* New York, NY: Sterling Publishing.

Deffenbacher, J. and Hazaleus, S. (1985) 'Cognitive, emotional, and physiological components of test anxiety.' *Cognitive Therapy and Research 9*, 169–180.

Dobson, R.L., Bray, M.A., Kehle, T.J., Theodore, L.A. and Peck, H.L. (2005) 'Relaxation and guided imagery as an intervention for children with asthma.' *Psychology in the Schools 42*, 7, 707–720.

Dubord, G. (2011) 'Part 12. Systematic desensitization.' *Canadian Family Physician 57*, 1299.

Ellis, A. (1961) *A Guide to Rational Living.* Englewood Cliffs, NJ: Prentice Hall.

Gladding, S. (2009) *Counseling: A Comprehensive Review* (6th edn). Upper Saddle River, NJ: Merrill/Pearson.

Gray, R. (2015) 'The art of healing and healing in art therapy.' *In Psych.* Retrieved 12 January 2018 from www.psychology.org.au/inpsych/2015/june/gray

Guest, J. (2016) *The CBT Art Activity Book.* London: Jessica Kingsley Publishers.

Harvey, L. Inglis, S.J. and Espie, C.A. (2002) 'Insomniacs' reported use of CBT components and relationship to long-term clinical outcome.' *Behaviour Research and Therapy 40*, 75–83. doi:10.1016/s0005-7967(01)00004-3

Henley, D. (2002) *Clayworks in Art Therapy: Plying the Sacred Circle*. London: Jessica Kingsley Publishers.

Hope, D.A., Burns J.A., Hyes S.A., Herbert J.D. and Warner, M.D. (2010) 'Automatic thoughts and cognitive restructuring in cognitive behavioral group therapy for social anxiety disorder.' *Cognitive Therapy Research 34*, 1–12.

Ilacqua, G.E. (1994) 'Migraine headaches: Coping efficacy of guided imagery training.' *Headache: The Journal of Head and Face Pain 34*, 99–102.

Ivey, A., D'Andrea, M., Ivey, M. and Simek-Morgan, L. (2002) *Theories of Counselling and Psychotherapy: A Multicultural Perspective*. Boston, MA: Pearson.

Kabat-Zinn, J. (2013) *Full Catastrophe Living: Using the Wisdom of Your Body and Mind to Face Stress, Pain, and Illness*. New York, NY: Random House.

Kanter, J.W., Schildcrout, J.S. and Kohlenberg, R.J. (2005) 'In vivo processes in cognitive therapy for depression: Frequency and benefits.' *Psychotherapy Research 15*, 366–373. doi:10.1080/10503300500226316

Larimer, M., Palmer, R. and Marlatt, G. (1999) 'Relapse prevention: An overview of Marlatt's cognitive-behavioral model.' *Alcohol Research and Health 23*, 2, 151–160. Retrieved 12 January 2018 from https://pubs.niaaa.nih.gov/publications/arh23-2/151-160.pdf

Laugeson, E.A. and Park, M.N. (2014) 'Using a CBT approach to teach social skills to adolescents with autism spectrum disorder and other social challenges: The PEERS Method.' *Journal of Rational-Emotive and Cognitive-Behavior Therapy 32*, 1, 84–97.

Lineham, M. (2015) *DBT Skills Training Manual*. New York, NY: Guilford.

Lowen, A. (1976) *Bioenergetics*. London: Penguin.

Lowenstein, L. (2016) *Creative CBT Interventions for Children with Anxiety*. Toronto: Champion Press.

Manning, J. and Ridgeway, N. (2016) *CBT Worksheets for Teenage Social Anxiety*. New York, NY: Createspace Independent Publishers.

Martin, R. and Dahlen, E. (2005) 'Cognitive emotion regulation in the prediction of depression, anxiety, stress, and anger.' *Personality and Individual Differences 39*, 1249–1260. doi:10.1016/j.paid.2005.06.004

McNeill, S. (2011) *Zen Mandalas: Sacred Circles Inspired by Zentagle*. East Petersburg, PA: Fox Chapel Publishing.

Mo [Screen name] (2010, 21 April) 'Bodily motions influence memory and emotions' [Blog post]. Science Blogs: Neurophilosophy. Retrieved 12 January 2018 from http://scienceblogs.com/neurophilosophy/2010/04/21/motions-influence-emotions

Perry, B.D. (n.d.) 'Self-regulation: The second core strength.' *Early Childhood Today*. Retrieved 12 January 2018 from http://teacher.scholastic.com/professional/bruceperry/self_regulation.htm

Pert, C. (1997) *Molecules of Emotion*. New York, NY: Simon and Schuster.

Rossman, M. (2010, 18 August) 'Relaxation and imagery, meditation, and hypnosis – What's the difference? Worry Solution: Using Breakthrough Brain Science to Turn Stress and Anxiety into Confidence and Happiness.' Retrieved 4 March 2017 from http://worrysolution.com/2010/08/18/relaxation-and-imagery-meditation-and-hypnosis%E2%80%94what%E2%80%99s-the-difference

Sherwood, P. (2000a) 'Beholding: Bridging the chasm between flooding and denial: Philophonetics counselling and sexual abuse survivors.' *Journal of the Incest Survivors Association*, September, pp.23–32.

Sherwood, P. (2000b) Bridging the chasm: Philophonetics counselling and healing the trauma of sexual abuse. *Diversity 2*, 4 18–25.

Sherwood, P. (2004) *The Healing Art of Clay Therapy*. Melbourne: Acer.

Sherwood, P. (2008) *Emotional Literacy: The Heart of Classroom Management*. Melbourne: Acer.

Sherwood, P. (2011) *Emotional Literacy: The Workbook*. Bunbury, W.A.: Sophia Publications.

Sherwood, P. and O'Meara, K. (2012) *Clay Therapy: Healing Rwandan Genocide*. Bunbury, W.A.: Sophia Publications.

Sherwood, P. and Tagar, Y. (2000a) 'Experience awareness tools for preventing burnout in nurses.' *Australian Journal of Holistic Nursing 7*, 1, 15–20.

Sherwood, P. and Tagar, Y. (2000b) 'Self-care tools for creating resistance to burnout: A case study in philophonetics counseling.' *Australian Journal of Holistic Nursing 7*, 2, 45–46.

Tagar, Y. (1996) *Philophonetics: Love of Sounds*. Melbourne: Persephone Publications.

Thich Nhat Hanh (1987) *The Miracle of Mindfulness*. Boston, MA: Beacon.

Utay, J. and Miller, M. (2006) Guided imagery as an effective therapeutic technique: A brief review of its history and efficacy research. *Journal of Instructional Psychology 33*, 1. Retrieved February 2017 from www.questia.com/library/journal/1G1-144014458/guided-imagery-as-an-effective-therapeutic-technique

Witkiewitz, K. and Marlatt, G.A. (2004) 'Relapse prevention for alcohol and drug problems.' *American Psychologist 59*, 4, 224–235.

Wolpe, J. (1958) *Psychotherapy by Reciprocal Inhibition*. Stanford, CA: Stanford University Press.

Index